A MARKETING ACTION PLAN

for the

GROWING BUSINESS

Second Edition

Shailendra Yyakarnam
John Leppard

Acknowledgements
To all the small businesses from which we learnt so much, to Kris Molle for typing and to Natalie Thomas for graphics.

Note. Masculine pronouns have been used in this book. This stems from a desire to avoid ugly and cumbersome language, and no discrimination, prejudice or bias is intended.

First published in 1995
Second edition 1999

Kogan Page Limited
120 Pentonville Road
London N1 9JN

British Library Cataloguing in Publication Data

A CIP record for this book is available from the British Library.

ISBN 0 7494 2649 7

Typeset by Jean Cussons Typesetting, Diss, Norfolk
Printed and bound in Great Britain by Clays Ltd, St Ives plc

Contents

Preface

We are heartened and flattered that the demand for this book justifies a new edition. From the outset it was our intention to write something that was, as one reviewer put it, 'Low on theorizing and high on practical application.' Moreover, we saw no point in peddling a rigid dictat which asserted that there is only one way to be successful. Real life does not work like that.

Instead, we leave it to the good sense of our readers to choose what is the right direction for their businesses, having first presented them with a range of possible options. In addition, unlike many other business books, we spell out the consequences of adopting a particular strategy in terms of its impact on finance and manpower.

However, when we first wrote this book it was aimed essentially at the small business. Therefore, imagine our surprise to learn that our readership extended into many larger companies. Not only that, but their feedback to us was highly complimentary. On reflection, we concluded that the important issue affecting any enterprize is not its size, but what is happening to it. The problem of choosing the right direction for the business and maximizing resources is at the heart of growth for *any* company.

Accordingly, we have modified this second edition slightly to reduce the emphasis on 'smallness' and instead we have stressed growth. Even so, we have remained true to our original concept, which was to cut through theory and buzz-words to arrive at easy to understand decisions that have to be made by those seeking growth and success.

We hope that, after reading this book, you will agree that not only did we achieve these objectives, but also that the experience proved to be a good investment of your time.

Shai Vyakarnam and John Leppard
London 1998

1

Taking Stock of Your Situation

BUSINESS DIRECTION: WHAT ARE THE CHOICES?

Nowhere is business life more real and volatile than at the helm of a growing business. In our experience, the early success of growth keeps managers focused on ensuring the delivery of their products and services to their customers and the cash flow to themselves. However, many firms bump up against a glass ceiling after a period of growth. They begin to wonder from where their sustainable growth will come and what future directions they should pursue.

The problem facing most growing companies is not the lack of opportunities, but the lack of resources, be they people, equipment, skills or money. Like water in a desert, the few precious assets they do have must be used wisely and not be allowed to dribble away unproductively.

This book will show how a growing company can harness its resources in such a way that it focuses on the best and most profitable opportunities, thereby swinging the odds of success more favourably in its direction. Of course, there is no easy and painless magic potion that can be used. As the pithy north country adage stresses, 'tha never gets owt for nowt'. However, the natural energy and resilience of most companies provide a good bridgehead from which to move forward. Regardless of their self-criticism or admissions of short-comings, the fact that they are still players in the tough business world suggests that they are doing something right, even if that 'something' is not always immediately clear to them. Our experience of working with businesses gives us the confidence to know that they will do nothing which does not make sense or have a relevance to their situation. Thus, what follows is based on ideas which have been tried, tested and found to work.

BUT MY COMPANY IS DIFFERENT!

Of course it is. All companies are unique because they take on the characteristics of those who run them. They are also shaped by the nature of their technology and the working environment which is provided. Having said this, there are also many similarities between different types of company when it comes to seeking growth.

As we will show, while two companies might be faced with similar problems, how they set about solving them is going to reflect upon their special, individual characteristics. Thus, the reason for starting this book with a stock-taking exercise is to enable the reader to move from generalizations, which might apply broadly to all companies, to specifics which apply obviously to his or her business. However, before moving on, a question.

WHAT IS IT YOU SEEK FROM RUNNING YOUR OWN BUSINESS?

The motivations for running a business can be many and varied. For some people it is as simple as providing continuity in the family business. Like a relay runner, they have taken the baton from the earlier generation and in time will pass it on to a younger successor. For them the main motivation might be to ensure that there is a business to pass on. Others might have started out with an idea they wanted to exploit; some might be in love with a particular technology; others perhaps need an outlet for their artistic talents. There will be some people who seek to maintain a particular life-style, while others are driven to make 'loads of money', to quote the vernacular.

Each and every one of these motives it quite legitimate, but it must be recognized that the underlying reason which drives the business is going to influence the way it is run. For example, a risk-taking entrepreneur might be inclined to pursue any opportunity which promises high returns. Someone who is running his or her business to provide a steady, if not spectacular, income, the so-called 'replacement income entrepreneur', is likely to be far more circumspect regarding risk-taking and opt for a more cautious growth pattern. Those running the family business might find themselves trapped by its previous history which, rather than providing options, actually appears to shut them down.

Thus, for one reason or another, most small companies will have one of the following broad strategies which reflects upon their particular circumstances:

- to survive
- to consolidate and tick over in much the same way
- to expand and grow.

However, on closer inspection it becomes self-evident that while on the surface these strategies might look different, they do in fact all boil down to the last one. The reason for claiming this becomes apparent if the model of the business (Figure 1.1) is taken into consideration.

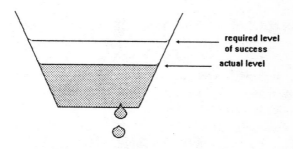

Figure 1.1 *The business bucket*

Any company can be likened to a bucket in that there is a level to which it must be filled with business in order to constitute success. To paraphrase that well-known Dickensian economist, Mr Wilkins Macawber, if the company can exceed this level it faces a rosy future, but should it fail then doom and despair await.

To provide a realistic model, the bucket is shown as having a hole in it. This represents the leakage that most businesses experience. This might be loss of profits, owing to wastage or errors being made in the business. Customers might cease trading with the business, leading to a loss of market share, or the lack of adequate emphasis on selling might just lead to lost opportunities. In general, growth companies keep this leakage to a minimum.

However, some businesses have to learn to live with a fairly fast-leaking bucket, for example, if they are selling items for which there is little likelihood of a repeat sale, as with double glazing. The only way for them to survive is to keep finding new customers to keep the level of business 'topped up'.

Extending the bucket analogy further, companies struggling to survive are faced with a situation where it is emptying faster than they can fill it. The answer? Find new customers or sell more to existing ones. Those companies who wish to tick over in a relatively trouble-free way must take care that they are not lulled into a false sense of security. For their bucket is also leaking and in order to keep business at the same level, they too will need to seek a modest level of growth. Rather like walking up a down escalator, energy has to be expended just to stay in the same place. It will be dangerous for those who fall into this category to lose sight of this principle.

Therefore, for a multitude of reasons, all companies must seek growth and expansion at some level, however modest, if only to stay where they are. The more bullish ones can drive themselves forward with far more challenging growth targets. Thus, the question that faces most companies is where and how they can seek sufficient growth, whether in profits or sales, to meet their needs? Closely related to this is how much effort they are prepared to devote to the task?

DREAMS AND REALITY

The other day we saw a postcard in a shop printed with one of those pungent, jokey messages which seem to be so popular nowadays. This is what it said:

> When you are up to your backside in
> alligators it is difficult to remember
> that the original objective was
> to drain the swamp.

In many different ways, but admittedly never quite as picturesquely, managers of growing businesses have expressed these same sentiments to us. Their once clear starting objectives have been overtaken by events, and in the process their original sense of direction has become temporarily (sometimes completely) lost. Such a loss of momentum can be fatal for a small company because unlike its larger counterpart it does not have the residual impetus that comes from its mass to keep it going.

It is therefore important to restore a sense of vision as the starting point for developing the business. Large companies have mission statements to guide them because they have to satisfy so many different stakeholders, the banks, key suppliers and so on. The smaller company can be driven by the owner's dream. After all, if the company cannot be used to satisfy the owner's dream, why run it? Perhaps the word dream is too woolly; what we are advocating is that the businessman establishes an image of the future which represents what he is hoping to achieve. This might be visualized in purely financial terms, such as becoming seriously rich, or it might be more fanciful such as retiring at a certain age and moving to Florida to play golf. However, the implication for this second type of vision is that somehow the wherewithal has been earned to make it all possible. Even life-style dreams cannot escape the financial realities of business.

For most of us, the present day reality falls far short of the image of the future we might hold. This being the case, the following technique can be used to help us see what steps we might have to take. At the end of the day the basis for a successful future is going to revolve around:

- matching personal and business goals
- organizing yourself in terms of skills
- building and managing relationships.

It sounds rather simple when stripped down to its basics. Can it really be that easy?

FORCE-FIELD ANALYSIS

This technique enables factors that are blocking progress to be identified (see Figure 1.2).

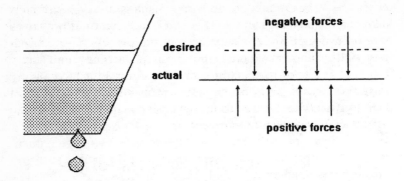

Figure 1.2   *The balance of opposing forces*

At any particular time, the actual level of the business bucket is the point of balance between all the positive things the company is trying to do to raise the level, and the negative things which are tending to lower it. The fact that business does not drain away completely is a testimony to the positive effort being expended.

If the businessman can identify the main forces which operate on his business as suggested by Figure 1.2, he is well on the way towards developing a strategy which will lead to improvement. In other words, he will get closer to filling the business bucket to its desired level.

At first sight it would appear that to increase the business level, it would be necessary to increase the positive forces while at the same time reducing the negative ones. In fact this is not the case (as Exercise 1.1 will demonstrate). In practice it always proves difficult to improve positive forces. Let us consider a few examples of such forces to prove this point:

- staff are highly motivated
- good relationship with the main customers
- excellent record on deliveries
- quality second to none.

Faced with such information what, for example, can be done to make highly motivated staff even more motivated? Or an excellent delivery record even better? The answer is: very little. In fact, tampering with already good performance levels might prove to be counter-productive.

The imperative from the analysis of the force field is that most effort must be applied to *reducing the negative forces*, thereby allowing the positive forces to make their full impact. However, the true influence of both the negative and positive forces can only be assessed by knowing the desired level the company is trying to achieve. The following exercise enables the reader to apply the force-field technique to his or her own business. Not only will it help to identify realistic goals for the business, but it will also highlight the target areas for improvement.

| Exercise 1.1 | **Selecting Targets for the Change Effort** |

Step 1

In order to confirm a sense of direction (assuming for the moment that you have strayed from your objectives while fighting off alligators), write down a sheet of paper what your long-term ambition/vision/dream is or was for yourself as achieved through the business. For example, to make money (how much?), to be able to retire in comfort (what does this mean to you?), to pass the business over to a son or daughter (in what state?), to sell the business (at what price?), to be doing much the same as now (at what size and level of sales?), to be respected in the area or in the industry (for doing what?).

Put a time scale against these objectives so that a further sense of realism is injected into the process.

Step 2

Now consider where you are today and how close you are to realizing your vision. Make a list of all the differences between now and then, for example, your income from the company, its size, its asset value, your life-style, its turnover, etc. Of course, because you are dealing in possibilities and not facts, any figures you come up with will only be approximate, but that does not matter at this stage.

Step 3

Visualize the coming year as a stepping stone towards achieving your long-term ambitions. Looking at the list generated in Step 2, set yourself end-of-year targets which will take you closer to your vision. Be as realistic as possible, yet set yourself challenging targets. This time any figures you use, although extrapolated from approximations, must be treated as real. You are now ready to develop a force-field analysis for your business.

Clearly, issues about life-style and finance are closely related, since one pays for the other. However, there can be elements of one's personal life which do not immediately equate to a cash sum. For example, making a decision to be more open with one's staff, learning to relax more. For this reason we recommend that two force-field diagrams are made.

Step 4

Develop two diagrams as shown (in Figures 1.3 and 1.4 below), adding all the relevant positive and negative forces. Note. Those shown below are just to provide examples.

Step 5

Study the two force-field diagrams and make a list of the key negative forces which need to be addressed in the coming year in order to reduce their impact. Of course, you may not be able to identify them all in isolation and may need to take advice from someone who knows you well and whose judgement you trust.

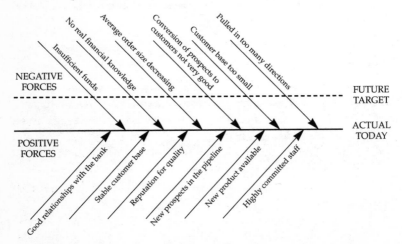

Figure 1.3   *Force field: Example applied to a fall in business*

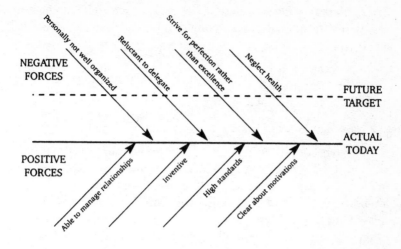

Figure 1.4 *Personal force field*

Now you can apply your knowledge and skills to deal with the forces through asking the following questions:

- What can be done to reduce the major negative forces?
- What might be done to produce some quick results?
- What might be done which is easiest and least costly?

Step 6

Draw up a simple action plan regarding the issues which it makes good sense to work on. As a general rule, precede each action with the format:

'By—(date)—I will need to have done—(action)—.'

In addition to providing you with ideas for an action plan, Exercise 1.1 will also have achieved two things which in academic parlance would have been called:

(a) Gap analysis, ie the difference between where you are and where you ought to be; and
(b) a fairly comprehensive analysis of the strengths and weaknesses of both you and your company which, to all intents and

purposes, equates to the same thing. Strengths and weaknesses form part of the so-called SWOT analysis which lies at the heart of organizational 'stock-taking'.

You may have developed a list of action items from this analysis. As we stated earlier, it may be more important to address the weaknesses first than to deal with the strengths you already have. The list of weaknesses may have highlighted day-to-day operational problems you face in the business, or as we call them, 'Opportunities For Errors'.

We have found numerous 'OFEs', for example: data being entered twice when orders are received, wrong assumptions being made about customer needs, lack of negotiation on purchasing, no attention being paid to energy consumption, job roles unclear, missed messages from clients and so forth. Most businesses are littered with them. You might find that a tough-minded pursuit in their reduction could release the very resources you need to grow your business. We know of several companies where a reduction of just two 'OFEs' has led to losses turning into significant profits.

The 'O' and 'T' components of SWOT come from considering the Opportunities and the Threats which face the company. How you can arrive at these is the subject of Exercise 1.2.

| Exercise 1.2 | **Identifying opportunities and threats** |

This exercise is intended neither to explore the reaches of 'never-never land', nor to look for bogeymen who do not really exist. It is designed to encourage you to make a calm and reasoned appraisal of your particular business world.

Step 1

Using personal experience of your markets and all that surrounds them, and taking on board the opinions of others which you value, make a list of things that are likely to happen in your business environment which could have beneficial effects on your fortunes.

Examples of where to look for opportunities might be to see what is happening to your customers, new technologies, competitors in difficulty, new premises becoming available at a convenient location, increased traffic due to road network, improvements in communication, social changes in fashion, home improvements and so on.

NOTE: two memory joggers or mnemonics might help you here. They are the acronyms:

- CESPIT, ie   Competition
    Economic cycles
    Social trends
    Political decision
    Institutions
    Technology
- Or PEST, ie   Political
    Economic
    Social
    Technological.

They both highlight some of the areas you might consider.

Step 2

Using a similar pragmatic approach, identify all those things on the horizon which could have a negative effect on your business.

Examples of threats might be that you are locked into one customer or one supplier; there are effective competitors or you don't know who they are; your key contact at a major customer is about to retire; interest rate changes will affect the level of stock that can be held; competition is moving to computers and you are not, and so on.

Step 3

Look back at both your lists and in each identify the top three items that:

- have an extremely high probability of happening; and
- have a potentially high impact on your business.

These are the major opportunities and threats which need to be considered in your thinking about the business. They can be thought of as those few things that need to be addressed for you to be effective, ie critical success factors.

You can now complete the SWOT analysis on your company by extracting the major Strengths, Weaknesses, Opportunities and Threats and entering them in the box below. You will be using the information in a little while. Of course, sometimes it is difficult to say whether a strength is actually a weakness or whether a threat can be turned into an opportunity. This ambiguity can be used to advantage as it sets you thinking about the issue. One possible way to try to identify whether something is a strength, weakness, opportunity or threat is to ask: **'So what does this mean to me?'**

STRENGTH	WEAKNESS
OPPORTUNITY	THREAT

Exercise 1.3	**Strategic options questionnaire**

The following questionnaire will help you to identify the main strategic options which you believe to be correct for your business. This questionnaire makes a number of statements, some of which might be quite accurate descriptions of your company. Your task is to consider each statement and circle the appropriate answer, according to this format:

0	1	2	3
Not at all descriptive	Partly descriptive	Reasonably descriptive	Highly descriptive

Before you start scoring the questionnaire, it is worth mentioning that you may not be able to answer all the questions straight away. In this case you should highlight these for further investigation or discussion with colleagues or advisers. It is important to answer all questions.

1. Regular customer base is generally shrinking — 0 1 2 3
2. Your product/service is easy to describe — 0 1 2 3
3. Your business is very specialized — 0 1 2 3
4. New technology and/or substitutes are outdating your current products — 0 1 2 3
5. You have only a few large organizations as customers — 0 1 2 3
6. You need a fresh challenge, frequently and personally — 0 1 2 3
7. There is high potential for more business from existing customers — 0 1 2 3
8. There would be higher margins on new products and services — 0 1 2 3
9. A key person has left your company and affected it critically — 0 1 2 3
10. The company is as big as you want it to be — 0 1 2 3
11. Your strengths are mainly technical — 0 1 2 3
12. Average order size is decreasing — 0 1 2 3
13. The existing products/services have passed their 'sell by date' — 0 1 2 3
14. You have good relationships with existing customers — 0 1 2 3
15. Your products/services could be standardized to give you cost savings — 0 1 2 3
16. Competition is killing you — 0 1 2 3
17. Your objectives are met by staying much the same — 0 1 2 3
18. Someone has offered to buy you out — 0 1 2 3
19. You can identify similarities among your customers — 0 1 2 3
20. It is fairly easy for you to develop new products and services — 0 1 2 3
21. There is a high demand for your current products and services — 0 1 2 3
22. A new collaborator has excellent contacts in another business field which interests you — 0 1 2 3
23. Your products/services are relatively new on the market — 0 1 2 3

24. You are an enthusiast   0 1 2 3
25. Competition is quite active in your current market   0 1 2 3
26. You are good at selling to customers   0 1 2 3
27. You have the capability to produce or find new
    products and services   0 1 2 3
28. You can see a better business opportunity   0 1 2 3
29. Existing customers are growing quite modestly   0 1 2 3
30. Your products/services do not lend themselves
    to repeat purchase   0 1 2 3
31. You have extensive knowledge about your
    existing customers (say three or more contacts
    at each one)   0 1 2 3
32. Your products/services are very competitive   0 1 2 3
33. You are good at developing new ideas   0 1 2 3
34. Your customer base is shrinking rapidly   0 1 2 3
35. Competition makes little impact on your business   0 1 2 3
36. Your products/services are beginning to look
    tired and dated   0 1 2 3
37. It is not feasible to expand in your situation   0 1 2 3
38. You have a super new idea   0 1 2 3
39. Existing demand is falling   0 1 2 3
40. You are not very good at managing change   0 1 2 3

Add your scores for the following statements and write the total in the boxes:

A		B		C		D	
3	...	4	...	1	...		...
	...	5	...	2	...	6	...
7	...	8	...		...	9	...
10	...	11	...	12	...	13	...
14	...		...	15	...	16	...
17	...	20	...	19	...	18	...
23	...	27	...	21	...	22	...
29	...	31	...	25	...	24	...
35	...	33	...	26	...	28	...
37	...	36	...	30	...	34	...
40	...	39	...	32	...	38	...

A = [   ]   B = [   ]   C = [   ]   D = [   ]

Transfer the scores into the boxes in Figure 1.5 below, in order to develop a picture of the best business direction to follow.

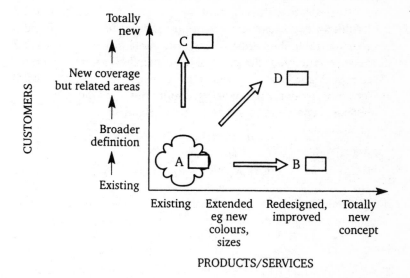

Figure 1.5 *Stay or move? The business directions map*

As Figure 1.5 shows, all business, whether large or small, is about getting products or services to customers. As the figure illustrates, customers can be perceived in a number of different ways, ranging from existing to totally new. Similarly, products or services can also be considered as current (existing) or an entirely new concept, with various degrees of modification and redesign in between.

Thus, the marketing options facing the company regarding which direction to take can be distilled down to four broad choices:

1. **Stay with existing customers and existing products/services. (Staying where you are)**

   This option may be one of choice or circumstance, but as long as you know this is where the business has to be, then action can be taken to maximize profitability. For example, companies like Hertz stay with existing customers (business people) with existing services (car rental) as a major operating strategy. They just try to do it better than others.

2. **Provide new products/services to existing customers. (Adding value to existing relationships)**

   Once a business has built up a stable customer base and has good relationships, one of the strategic options is to see what else you can sell to contacts built up with customers. It may be possible to add other services, offer new products, or find new ways of doing business which add value to the sale. Travel agents might offer theatre bookings for their clients; a petrol station might start to sell groceries or second-hand cars; computer software companies could offer upgrades to their existing clients, and so on.

3. **Provide existing products/services to new customers. (Finding new customers with what you have)**

   In situations where repeat sales are unlikely, it is essential to keep finding new customers, as indeed is the desire to build market share and dominate a market niche. In this situation the product offering remains basically the same, but may be tuned to local market conditions. An example of when this was **not** done was the launch of EuroDisney when the senior managers believed that the totally American formula could be plonked directly into France. EuroDisney now offers wine, thus breaking its non-alcoholic principle which operates in the USA.

4. **Provide new products and services to new customers. (Diversification)**

   In situations where the products have died away or the customer base has suddenly disappeared, or indeed if the business is cash rich, it may be possible to enter new markets with new products. Having said that, this is one of the more risky strategies as you might be going into new territory without the requisite knowledge and experience, either of the products or the markets. Recent examples of diversification away from the core business include the farming community who have to shift from farming to non-farm activity as a means of survival. On the large company front, a typical diversification might be a cash-rich tobacco company going into life assurance.

In general, the growing company must focus on just one of the strategic directions for a given time-frame because its relative lack of resources denies it the luxury of spreading its options. In other words, if it tries to spread itself over too wide a business spectrum, its impact will be greatly diminished, if not cause its demise.

The significance of selecting any one of these options is far reaching because it can determine much of what happens to the company thereafter, from policy-making to dealing with day-to-day issues. The full impact of each of these different options will be considered in greater detail later in this book. For now it is enough to be clear about which is the best business direction for your company by making a conscious choice, rather than by drift or force or circumstance.

Staying where you are (A)

If your highest score in the Strategic Options Questionnaire was for box A, it suggests that to stay with existing customers and products or services could be your best choice of action. Thus, you should focus on Chapter 2 for action planning.

Selling new products to existing customers (B)

If your highest score was for box B, this suggests that your most favourable business direction could be to provide new products or services to your existing customers and you should focus on Chapter 3 for action planning.

Finding new customers for existing products (C)

If box C was your highest score, this points towards finding new customers or groups of customers for your existing products or services and Chapter 4 has guidance on action planning for this option.

Diversification (D)

Finally, box D will indicate that diversification from finding new products or services for new customers could be the best course of action to pursue and you should focus on Chapter 5 for action planning.

BUSINESS DIRECTION

The purpose of all the preceding exercises was to help establish the nature of the launch pad from which business will go forward. The keys to success have been found to be:

- the company plays to its strengths
- it seeks the best opportunities/business strategies
- it tries to remedy or side-line its weaknesses
- it tries to side-step and thus avoid potential threats
- above all, the entrepreneur and his or her team are highly committed to the route it is planned to take.

Time and time again we have found that businesses which operate with these five elements in place have established a winning formula. Of course, like life in general, some just happened to be in the right place at the right time. However, it would be wrong to ascribe luck to most growth company success stories. They were achieved by hard work and an instinct for doing the right things in the right way.

From what has gone before, you are now in possession of your:

- Strengths   S
- Weaknesses   W
- Opportunities   O
- Threats   T

You have also considered your ultimate destination (what you really want from your business) and what targets you must set to start out on the journey. However, as with any journey, the route you choose to reach your destination can be critical. In real life we can use motorways, arterial roads, country lanes or public transport systems. In business life we are faced with similar options regarding the best route to take. The Strategic Options Questionnaire tries to outline what these possibilities are, but naturally, a fairly simple paper and pencil exercise cannot replicate all the complexity of the business world. Nevertheless, this questionnaire ought to provide some important clues about your best business direction, if not the complete answer.

Having said this, the questionnaire results, coupled with the SWOT analysis and your personal knowledge and expertise, ought collectively to give you the confidence to choose the business direction best suited to your circumstances.

As illustrated in Figure 1.6, what you are looking for is overlap, consistency and mutual support from these analyses of yourself and your business. It is also quite possible that the scores for all four options will be so close that a clear choice does not emerge. If this is

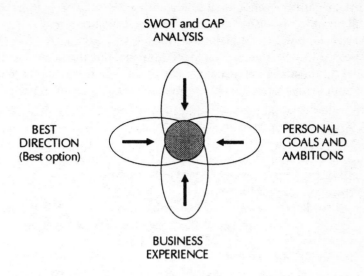

Figure 1.6 *Getting the best business overlap*

the case, further thinking may be required, primarily to choose one main option in order to make best use of limited resources.

APPLICATION ACTIVITIES

1. If you have only tackled the exercises in this chapter in a superficial way, please look back at them more seriously because they do yield important information.
2. Analyse all the data from the exercises and combine this with your commercial experience to arrive at the best business direction option for your company.

SUMMARY

In this opening chapter we made a case for claiming that while all businesses are unique in many ways, they are also similar in that they are faced with limitless possibilities, but finite and scarce resources. Since the motivation for running a business can differ from one person to another, it followed that the way each attempts to fill his or her particular business 'bucket' can also differ.

However, because all businesses have a leakage which is represented by lost customers, lost opportunities and inefficiencies, in reality all must strive for an element of growth just to stay where they are. Where such growth originates depends partly on where the business person wants to go (dreams) and to what extent he or she is tied to existing circumstances (reality). The technique of force-field analysis was introduced to throw light upon the key factors which helped or hindered the business from taking off. By planning to reduce the impact of the negative forces on the business, it was possible to select specific improvement targets.

Even so, it was necessary to examine in greater detail the gap between the current financial circumstances of the business and what they needed to be in order to constitute success. This necessitated completing a SWOT analysis and a Strategic Options Questionnaire which indicated the most favourable business direction to follow.

Finally, we showed how these various forms of analysis, which provide different kinds of insight, can be integrated to enable the business person to make a conscious choice about the future direction of the company. Whether that final choice is:

- staying where you are
- adding value to existing relationships
- finding new customers with what you have, or
- diversification.

It helps the company to focus its scarce resources in the most productive way. Moreover, the chosen business direction has a fundamental impact on the subsequent policies, staffing and operating procedures of the company, as the forthcoming chapters will illustrate.

2

Staying the Same: Selling Existing Products to Existing Customers

INTRODUCTION

In order to read this chapter, the 'stock-taking' of the business outlined in Chapter 1, in particular the outcome of the exercises, should have pointed towards staying much the same as a business option on the 'directional map'.

This particular option, like any of the other options, has its advantages and disadvantages. From the outset it is important for the business person to be aware of what these might be because they will loom large over how the company is managed and influence which key issues need to be monitored and controlled. This chapter will examine all of these in some detail.

CHOICE OR CHANCE?

That the business person finds him or herself in this particular area of the business direction map might be either through choice or chance. Some people perhaps see no way to escape from this strategic position. They can voice many good reasons for feeling trapped. Here are just some of them.

No time to change

For someone who is perhaps approaching retirement, the prospect of changing the nature of the business will hold no high attraction. Instinctively, it will be sensed that all the effort will not be worth while unless of course there is somebody to whom the business will be passed.

Caught in a skills trap

It is not easy for someone to abandon their hard-earned skills and expertise. For good or bad, they carried the business to its present position and largely dictate what can and cannot be accomplished by the company. In all probability, the violin maker, the architect, the potter, the accountant and the printer will continue doing what they do best, even though an outstanding alternative business opportunity might be staring them in the face ... and who could say they were wrong?

Dictated to by the situation

Some businesses find they cannot change even if they want to. Factors beyond their control force them to continue in more or less the same vein. For example, there is the farmer who is being encouraged to grow less in order to reduce the so-called food mountains. If he tried to sell the land for housing there might be all kinds of problems with local authorities, as indeed there might be if he tried to put up a golf course. It might also be pertinent to ask what else he might do to earn income if he did less farming? This leaves him with no choice other than to plough on, both literally and metaphorically.

Enmeshed with existing customers

Some businesses are so tied to their existing customers that they would find it difficult to break away even if they wanted. Sometimes the ties might be contractual ones, but more often than not they are because of a mutual dependency which has built up over the years.

Lack of capital

One of the biggest reasons for companies to adopt a 'stay much as we are' strategy is that they do not have the funds to do otherwise. Without being able to invest in new technology, or move to larger premises, they are hamstrung in terms of choosing new options.

However, being 'trapped' in this strategic position is not necessarily all bad news; there can be some distinct advantages for the company.

THE ADVANTAGES OF STAYING MUCH THE SAME

1. It is the natural thing to do

If they were honest, deep down most people would own up to the fact that while they recognize that change is taking place all around, given the opportunity, they would prefer things to stay much the same. Indeed, most of us organize our lives into routines and relationships which are designed to provide stability. Having a sameness in our personal world provides a haven of predictability in a seemingly turbulent and, at times, hostile ocean of change.

That such a choice is wise and legitimate is endorsed by adages such as 'better the devil you know than the devil you don't', 'a cobbler should stick to his last' and 'if something's not broke then don't try to mend it'. Thus, there is a stream of consciousness or accumulated wisdom in the human psyche which tells us that we will be most comfortable staying where we are. Even references to 'grass being greener on the other side' implies that change is an attractive and seductive illusion which never lives up to its promise.

2. Risks are minimized

By staying much the same, with existing products/services and customers, there is none of the associated risks of developing new products and finding new customers. Sometimes the lure of finding new customers leaves existing ones feeling somewhat neglected with reduced levels of services and satisfaction. You might risk losing a good thing while searching for the new product or customer. There is much truth in the old proverb that ... 'a bird in the hand is worth two in the bush'.

3. Expertise can be developed

The more you work at delivering the same products or services, the more expert you become. If you were continually switching from one thing to another there would be less opportunity to develop skills and experience in the same way, because people would be continually having to relearn the work. This is why a professional decorator can hang wallpaper faster than a DIY enthusiast. The former is doing the job every day, whereas the latter may have gaps of two years or so before he does the job again.

4. Costs are minimized

As expertise is developed and the business stays focused on known factors, all wasteful elements of cost can be eliminated. For example, there will be less scrap or rework and regular purchasing of raw materials may lead to special discounts. In addition, research shows that on average it costs *five times less* to sell to existing customers than to new ones. The savings come from reduced prospecting and non-productive administrative tasks such as credit checking.

5. Existing customers are less price sensitive

If the business has been supplying the same customers for a number of years, it follows that its customers must value the total package it provides. Because they know they receive good value and service from a trusted supplier, they are unlikely to raise eyebrows if prices are increased in recognition of enhanced product performance. In contrast, new customers invariably seek a supplier with the keenest prices.

6. The company can become known

Because the company is doing business over time with the same customers, with the same products or services, it can develop a unique reputation. Whether or not this is achieved mainly through its product quality or the nature of relationships is of secondary importance to the fact that the company is known and recognized.

However, while these advantages are undoubtedly real, there can also be clouds on the horizon.

DISADVANTAGES OF STAYING WITH EXISTING PRODUCTS AND CUSTOMERS

1. There might not be sufficient growth potential in the market

As stated in Chapter 1, the notion of staying exactly the same is illusory. In real life there is always an element of leakage from the 'business bucket' and, even if inflation runs at a modest level, the business must still strive to keep up with it. Thus, the existing bank of customers must be capable of yielding sufficient business potential into the future.

2. Are markets sufficiently stable?

Another potential danger for companies staying where they are relates to the stability of their markets. If their customers' businesses are under threat, or if ordering patterns are haphazard, in terms of order size or frequency, or if new suppliers threaten to burst upon the scene, the whole business structure might prove to be too unstable to rely on.

3. The products/services might not have sufficient life left in them

Just as the customer bank might lack the potential to sustain sufficient growth, so might a similar fault be attributed to the products or services. All company outputs eventually begin to show their age when matched against newer offerings. Those that are nearing the end of their expected life, or those that are threatened by new fashions, new technology or even proposed changes in legislation, are clearly not going to have the staying power to sustain the business into the future.

4. Complacency

A distinct disadvantage of the 'no change' strategy is that the company will not face the stimuli that change provides. Without being stretched to be creative, or being forced to rise to a new challenge, complacency might set in, with all its attendant dangers.

5. Trapped by the status quo

Working in a particular market means adapting to the characteristics that pass as norms for that kind of business. Thus, quality standards, prices and profit margins, three key ingredients for company health, become geared to the expectations of a specific group of existing customers. This could mean that even if an exciting new business opportunity came along, the company might find itself unable to be competitive because of the 'mind set' imposed by its traditional customers. In other words, it might miss the opportunity of establishing business with new customers where, for example, quality standards were less demanding and there was a potential for charging far higher prices.

It is clear from this consideration of the advantages and disadvantages that choosing a strategy to sell existing products or services to existing customers requires the businessman to have an intimate knowledge of the customers, while at the same time ensuring that what is offered remains competitive. What follows will focus on customers and products and, since a business's fortunes are closely tied to those of its customers, we will start with them.

ANALYSING THE CUSTOMERS

Rather like the saying, 'all people are equal, but some are more equal than others', it would be true to state that all customers are important but some more so than others. So who are the important customers and what is known about them?

80/20 rule

Customer sales can be analysed according to an empirical rule known as Pareto's Law, or more commonly the 80/20 rule. This observation-based rule operates as shown in Figure 2.1.

If the sales of pop records were being analysed it would be found that the sales revenue of the No 1 hit far outscores that of the No 2. (This is why, in addition to the fame associated with reaching the top spot, it is also so extremely valuable for financial reasons). The second best seller is similarly that much better than the third, and so on, as Figure 2.1 illustrates.

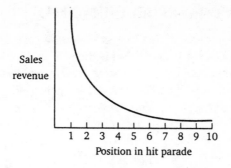

Figure 2.1 *Typical sales curve (pop records)*

Thus, the collective sales of the top two or three records account for the bulk of total sales. It has been found that approximately 20 per cent of the items sold in any range generate roughly 80 per cent of the total revenue. The remaining 80 per cent of items collectively account for 20 per cent of income. It is this proportionality which gave rise to the name 80/20 rule; however, it could equally be the 75/25 or perhaps even the 70/30 rule in some kinds of business.

Although the example is for pop records, the same curve would materialize with the analysis of any company sales records, so that if invoices were piled up in trays representing each customer, something like Figure 2.2 would emerge.

Clearly, with such a high dependency on a relatively small 20–30 per cent of the customer base, it is important that excellent working relationships are developed and maintained with these key customers. This entails recognizing what constitutes the decision-making unit at each of them.

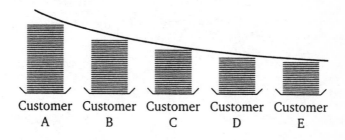

Figure 2.2 *Pile of invoices for top five clients*

The decision making unit (DMU)

Whenever a purchase is made it is generally easy to identify who constitutes the buyer because that is the person who signs the order and passes over money or a cheque. However, that person is not always the one who has the greatest influence on the decision to buy. This is particularly true when the sale is made to another company. In the context of a commercial sale, the buyer might be merely a cipher who is authorized to purchase up to a certain level. So, for example, if the supplying company was selling injection-moulded plastic components, it is likely that a number of people would be involved in the purchase decision. Moreover, each would be interested in a particular aspect of the bought-in component, see Figure 2.3.

The buyer himself might be a non-technical person to whom the component is nothing more than an expensive piece of plastic. His main concerns are likely to be to work within his budget and to secure a trustworthy source of supply which will not cause problems in the future. However, as Figure 2.3 shows, there are other

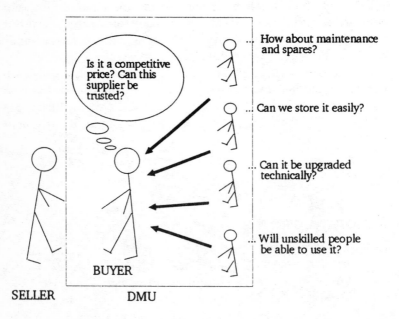

Figure 2.3   *The seller, the buyer and the DMU*

figures lurking in the background whose concerns go much deeper in terms of the quality and ultimate design of the component. They, too, make an impact on the buying decision in ways suggested by the diagram.

From the seller's point of view, he will be most effective and influential if he can meet and satisfy the demands of each member of the DMU. Sensible though this strategy appears to be, research shows that on average the seller only meets one or two people in the buying organisation. In other words, he never reaches some of the key figures who influence the decision to buy. Therefore, for the small businessman who is interested in developing relationships with the 20 per cent of key customers two issues emerge:

- the DMU must be identified
- members of each DMU must be met in order to understand their concerns and how the product or services might be tailored to be more attractive to them.

This is not quite as easy as it sounds because people do not go around wearing badges proclaiming that they are members of the DMU. Nor for that matter can job titles be an automatic guide to a person's role in the buying process. Sometimes a most unlikely figure can be the one to exert the most internal influence. None the less, by talking to people and generally doing some detective work it is possible to identify the key figures in the buying process.

Exercise 2.1	**Developing the decision-making unit (DMU)**

The importance of identifying each member of the DMU has been covered. This exercise is designed to build on this important idea.

Action steps

1. Focus on one of your major customers and make a note of the people you consider to be members of the DMU.

    Note. You might find it useful to consider the following piece of research. This indicates that as an organization gets larger, the DMU also increases. It also demonstrates that generally not all the members of the DMU are contacted, just one or two of them.

No of employees	Average no in DMU	Average no of contacts made
0– 200	3.42	1.72
201– 400	4.85	1.75
401–1000	5.81	1.90
1000+	6.50	1.85

2. Complete the form shown below, scoring each DMU member from 0 to 4 depending on the accuracy of each statement.

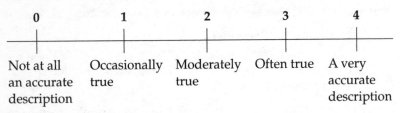

0	1	2	3	4
Not at all an accurate description	Occasionally true	Moderately true	Often true	A very accurate description

Note. If your first response to any statement is 'don't know', take steps to find out.

Members of DMU (insert names in boxes). Most important in box 1, thereafter in declining order of importance					
DMU member	**1**	**2**	**3**	**4**	**5**
Statement					
1. Is aware of me and the company					
2. Is aware of our product/service					
3. Understands how products/ services will help					
4. Believes in the product/service					
5. Supports us 100%					
6. Has a specialist need					
7. It has been demonstrated how specialist need can be met					
8. General relationship is good					

3. Study the completed form above, paying particular attention to the low scores, especially when they appear in columns to the left.
4. Make some notes about how you can develop relationships with the DMU, ie how and where scores can be made higher.

BUILDING A RELATIONSHIP

In some ways building a relationship between the supplier and the buyer can be likened to a personal relationship between a male and female. First, there is a courtship period where the two become acquainted. If this phase is successfully completed the relationship gradually becomes more legalized as engagement then marriage take place. After the honeymoon period both partners get down to making the relationship work in a steady and stable way. However, such is life that one may get bored with the other or feel let down, and take their affections elsewhere. Alternatively, both may spend many happy years together.

The reasons for giving this fanciful image of the relationship building process is to point out that both parties need to proceed at a pace which is acceptable to the other. There is no point in one party wanting to get married while the other is still at the courting stage. Indeed, a mismatch of expectations at any stage can lead to misunderstandings which could materialize as lost business.

A more rational model for relationship building was provided by two Americans, Joe Luft and Harry Ingham, in the 1960s. Their names are immortalized in the seemingly mystic title they gave their model.

The Johari Window

Luft and Ingham identified four component parts in the relationship between two people, the combination of which has a profound impact on the overall quality of the relationship. These components are as follows:

● The *open* part of the relationship where both parties are prepared to disclose and share information about themselves, their feelings and their values. This is where all the business is done because it is the only part of the relationship where both parties share information. Good relationships are found to have a very large open component.

- The *blind spot*, where one party is oblivious of something which is known to the other. This is like the 'bad breath' situation, where the culprit stays quite ignorant of the fact unless a well-meaning friend tells him or her.
- The *facade*, where one party deliberately keeps information from the other, for example, for fear of appearing to be weak or in order to establish a 'political' disadvantage.
- The genuinely *unknown* element of the relationship. This always exists and accounts for the fact that even in a long-standing relationship, one partner can do something which surprises the other, something of which they were not thought capable.

Diagrammatically, the Johari Window can be shown as in Figure 2.4:

SUPPLIER

	knows	doesn't know
knows	OPEN AREA	BLIND SPOT
doesn't know	FACADE	UNKNOWN

BUYER

Figure 2.4   *The Johari Window*

As was implied above, the significance of the 'window' is not that the four components exists, but how their relative sizes influence the overall relationship. Because relationships are capable of growing and developing, so can the Luft and Ingham model demonstrate how this can happen; see Figures 2.5 and 2.6.

The first of these 'windows' (Figure 2.5) shows a relationship at an early stage. It is characterized by a very large unknown and small open area. In contrast to this, the productive relationship has a

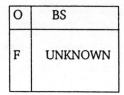

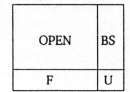

Figure 2.5 *Relationship at early stage not very productive*

Figure 2.6 *Productive relationship*

large open area and the unknown has reduced considerably. (*Note.* In both diagrams the blind spot and facade remain much the same size because others will never tell us everything about ourselves, and we always wish to keep a bit of ourselves private.)

What happens to change the relationship in Figure 2.5 to that shown in Figure 2.6? Clearly the 'crosswires' of the model have shifted ... but how? Think about it for a moment; what causes them to move?

Well, to move the vertical 'wire', the businessman must seek more feedback. This can be about how the product or service performs, what his company is like to do business with, what he could do to improve service, and so on. By seeking such information the blind spot grows progressively smaller.

The horizontal 'wire' can be similarly displaced if the businessman learns the skills of disclosure, that is to say, being more open with his contact. Such disclosure might include owning up to worries about some of the customer's requirements, sometimes asking for advice, coming clean about delivery problems, and so on.

However, as we said earlier, a relationship has to unfold at a rate which is appropriate for both parties if it is to reach the productive level of Figure 2.6. If it is rushed, results like those shown in Figures 2.7 and 2.8 are likely to come about.

To overwork disclosure skills means that the businessman comes across as verbose, arrogant, pushy, boastful and, of course, completely insensitive ... but he will never know this; just look at the size of the blind spot (Figure 2.7) The other party will eventually resent being talked at and never listened to, so the relationship will flounder.

To rely entirely on feedback also introduces a distortion into the relationship. For someone to be so apparently self-engrossed, as in the example shown in Figure 2.8, is in the end highly counter-

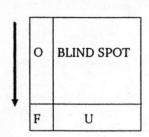

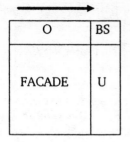

Figure 2.7 *Supplier overdoes disclosure*

Figure 2.8 *Buyer overdoes feedback*

productive. The person is seen as a mystery figure hiding behind a huge facade and ultimately as someone not to be trusted.

Some people, because of their personality type or upbringing, often have one of the skills of either getting feedback or disclosure more developed than the other. If they are to build good relationships they must learn perhaps to curb their natural inclinations and use both the skills in a more balanced way. This means that disclosure and receiving feedback must take place at a similar rate, thus keeping the open area predominantly square shaped. Or, to put it another way, ensuring that the blind spot or facade does not become unduly large. This is the enduring message of the Johari Window.

MEASURING RELATIONSHIPS: THE SPIDERGRAM

One way to measure the quality of your relationship is to list your customers and ask two questions, the first being, 'What is the current quality of relationship?' and the second, 'What should it be?' In answering the first question you should consider whether you know all the people involved in the buying decision, how they buy and why. Do you know how much they spend on your products and services as a proportion of total spend? For example, a small company with sales of £20,000 per year was very satisfied with its relationship, but when it found that the customer was only buying 10 per cent of their needs from the company, when they reassessed the relationship and realized there was a much higher potential. They increased sales to £40,000 without alerting competition to the encroachment.

One important factor in assessing the relationship must include profitability.

- Is the customer a profitable one to deal with?
- Is the company easy to deal with or so demanding that any profit is wiped out in higher costs?
- Do you sell to the customer at a comfortable profit margin?
- Does he or she pay on time?
- How financially secure is the customer?

If you do not have ready answers to these questions, the first exercise you will need to do is to analyse each customer carefully. You can then proceed with the spidergram in detail. You can also use the spidergram (see Figure 2.9) as an intuitive tool to get you started with the analytical process.

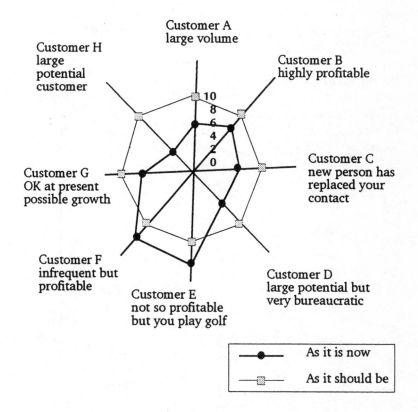

Figure 2.9 *Example spidergram of relationships*

The illustrative spidergram can also be used to measure relationships with bankers, suppliers, shareholders etc, to focus attention on those organizations or individuals who are likely to have a significant impact on the business. The gap between the current position and where the relationships should be helps to point out the areas for action.

It must never be overlooked, however, that while it is important to build productive relationships with the key customers (and the members of the DMU therein), the businessman must also pay attention to the products and services he provides. It is these that ultimately generate the revenue that the business needs if it is to thrive.

The following exercise will help you to quantify the value of key customers and to help to identify where attention must be focused.

Exercise 2.2 | Customer sales review

1. Make a list of customers to whom you have been selling over the last three years. For each year indicate the units sold and/or revenue for each customer.

Customers	Last year		Year before		Year before that	
	Volume (units)	Value £	Volume (units)	Value £	Volume (units)	Value £

2. Calculate what percentage of sales were generated from:

Government departments   _____
*Direct to end users   _____
Sold through intermediaries   _____
Sold to OEMs (Original
Equipment Manufacturers)   _____
*Exports   _____

TOTAL   **_____**

*It may be more useful or helpful to break down these figures
further. For example:
Geographical
Industry or segment
Use of application

ANALYSING PRODUCTS AND SERVICES

There has been oblique reference to this point before, but it must be
clearly understood that when customers buy a product or service
they are also 'buying' into a relationship with the supplying
company. In fact, rather than purchasing an item, they do in fact buy
a total package as Figure 2.10 shows.

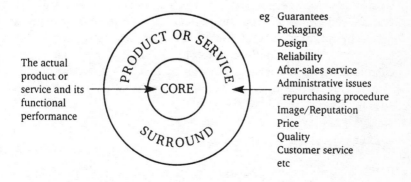

The actual
product or
service and its
functional
performance

eg Guarantees
Packaging
Design
Reliability
After-sales service
Administrative issues
  repurchasing procedure
Image/Reputation
Price
Quality
Customer service
etc

Figure 2.10 *The product/service as a total package*

Just as the 80/20 rule worked for analysing customers, so it does for analysing the 'product package'. It can be shown that providing the core product or service can account for something like 80 per cent of the costs, yet make only 20 per cent of the total impact on customers. In contrast, the product surround accounts for only 20 per cent of the costs yet makes 80 per cent of impact. In other words, customers are attracted mainly by the 'sizzle' and not the 'sausage'.

This bold statement needs to be qualified in that the core product performance *must* deliver what customers expect, but assuming this to be the case, any competitive edge or added value comes from redesigning the product surround. Not only does this make more impact but, just as importantly, it costs less. Moreover, as many competing products or services begin to look almost indistinguishable from one another, the businessman is driven to latch on to something like providing better customer service in order to establish an element of uniqueness in what he offers. Again this reinforces what we said earlier about identifying what the various members of the DMU look for in the product or service. Invariably, adjustments can be made to the customer package, tailoring it more specifically to the user's needs, thereby locking the customer ever more closely to the supplier.

The smaller company has major advantages over its larger competitors owing to the fact that all customers know the 'boss' and in all probability will have met him or her. Therefore there is a tremendous opportunity to cement this personalized relationship by backing it up with quality customer service. Not only can the smaller company respond swiftly to changing customer needs, but equally the customers can be persuaded that they are not mere names or numbers but that each received 'individual' attention. For their part, larger suppliers seek to become more flexible and customer friendly, but are often denied this by the nature of their bureaucratic procedures and sometimes monolithic organizational structures.

Analysing the products

It is well established and easily understood that all products or services have a finite life. Moreover, such a life cycle can be shown to follow the typical pattern illustrated in Figure 2.11.

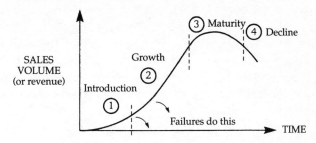

Figure 2.11 *Typical life cycle curve*

Initially there is the introduction phase, where sales are not very high, mainly because the new product or service is largely unknown, or the concept behind it has yet to win large-scale acceptance. Of course, many new offerings never do win the approval of customers and finish in the organizational 'dustbin'. (It is estimated that something like 90 per cent of new products fail to live up to expectations.) However, once the product is established in the eyes of customers the introduction phase gives way to a period of rapid growth, which naturally enough is called the growth phase. Eventually, most of the customers who are interested in the product or service have their needs satisfied by it and sales begin to level off. When this happens the so-called maturity phase has been reached. If no action is taken, sales decline as the final life phase is reached. Here, although much sadness might be associated with killing off an earlier breadwinner, a decision has to be made when the resources allocated to the virtually moribound product or service would be better used elsewhere, ie on something capable of generating greater sales. Exactly when to pull the plug on such an item is a matter of management judgement, but clearly something else must be available to take its place.

Just as we can undergo surgery and thereby have life extended, much the same can be done to products and services, see Figure 2.12. As the growth phase begins to peter out, it is sometimes possible to revamp the product or service in some way, thereby, quite literally, giving it a new lease of life.

In Figure 2.12, as sales start to decline at point A the supplier might, for example, offer the product in new colours. At point B, he might choose to introduce some new sizes into the product range.

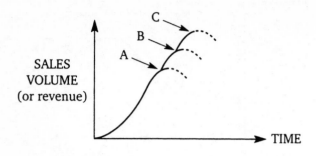

Figure 2.12 *Extending the life of products or services*

At point C, he might offer the product in new packaging or with a design modification which makes it more attractive, and so on. The underlying point with product life-extension strategies is that they cannot go on forever, but they can buy the company valuable time in which to develop a new product. Ideally, a company should be managing its products or services so that one begins to fade away at the very time that another is just beginning to take off. In this way sales are sustained and continual growth can be experienced.

Criticism of the life cycle concept

While the above description of the life cycle is undoubtedly true and can provide some valuable insights for the supplying company, which in turn can influence pricing, promotion and new product development, it is notoriously difficult for small companies (and many larger ones for that matter) to plot an accurate graph. What they actually record is not the product's life, but their management of it, see Figure 2.13.

Graph (a) is the 'true' total projected life cycle for a particular product or service, whereas graph (b) is the curve recorded by an individual company. Of course, the vertical scale of these graphs are of different dimensions, but it is the general shapes which are important, especially as both are on the same time-scale.

The company would, in isolation, conclude that the product in question had reached maturity. In fact, as Figure 2.12 shows, if total sales of the product are taken into account, it is really in its growth

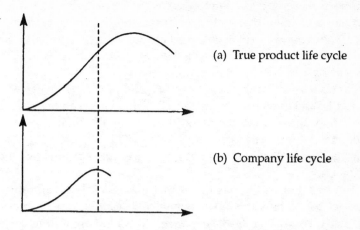

(a) True product life cycle

(b) Company life cycle

Figure 2.13 *'Misreading' the life cycle*

phase. In other words, somehow the company is failing to seize the true potential of the product. For its sales to be levelling off while total sales for that type of product are growing rapidly suggests that something is going very wrong. Clearly, the product is not competitive *as presently managed*.

However, even this reasonable analysis could be distorted because it would depend upon what was taken as the total sales figure and how the total life cycle was constructed, see Figure 2.14.

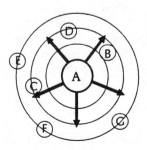

Figure 2.14 *What total sales?*

Suppose a disease started in town A as shown in Figure 2.14 and, by chance, a chemist there stumbled upon the cure. As soon as the word got round, sales would rocket, but then as people became cured or developed immunity, the chemist's medicine would be in increasingly less demand.

Even so, by now the disease would have spread to other towns B, C and D, and even further afield to E, F and G. Assuming chemists there had now gained the secret of the cure, the total sales of the medicine would show an astonishing growth rate, while the original chemist in town A could rightly claim that the product was now in decline.

The moral of this fairy story is that the life cycle of a product is also related to how the businessman chooses to define his market. The chemist trading solely in town A would show a different life cycle for the medicine from another chemist who was prepared to win customers in towns further away. Therefore, the product life cycle can be related to:

- the product's life
- how it is managed
- how the market is defined.

Exercise 2.3 | Product sales review

1. In the first instance there is a need to make a list of products and/or services which have been sold over the last three years. For each year indicate the units sold and/or revenue for each product/service.

Products/ Services	Last year		Year before		Year before that	
	Volume (units)	Value £	Volume (units)	Value £	Volume (units)	Value £

2. Calculate what percentage of sales were generated from:

Government departments   _____
*Direct to end users   _____
Sold through intermediaries   _____
Sold to OEMs (Original
Equipment Manufacturers)   _____
*Exports   _____

TOTAL   _____

*It may be more useful or helpful to break down these figures
further. For example:
Geographical
Industry or segment
Use of application

Life cycle applied to relationships with key customers

Since the reader of this chapter has a business which is primarily
selling an existing product or service to existing customers *and*, as
we established earlier, a key success factor is the quality of relationships with these customers, it is worth treating the relationship as
the 'product'. In other words, plot the life cycle of sales to those few
important customers who constitute the vital 20 per cent. Typical
results would be like those shown in Figure 2.15.

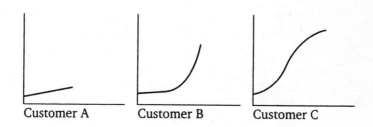

Figure 2.15 *Typical sales (relationship) life cycle*

With customer A, things are clearly at the introductory phase. In
these circumstances the company would be advised to do more to
establish credibility and to be accepted. Part of this strategy might
also include modifying the core product or service so that it meets

the customer's needs more adequately. Thus, some investment will be required.

With customer B, sales are still showing a healthy growth. The issues facing the company are therefore how to guarantee consistent supplies at the desired quality, and how to minimize costs and thereby increase profit margins.

With customer C, the relationship is reaching maturity with no prospect of the earlier growth phase being repeated. Here the businessman would be advised to try to re-energize sales by product modification (but only addressing the product surround, thereby achieving quick results at minimal costs). Since sales are unlikely to increase, it is important to maximize margins by minimizing costs.

By recognizing the essence of the relationship, as monitored through the business connection, the company is therefore in a position to adopt the best strategy which matches the circumstances.

CRITICAL SUCCESS FACTORS

There are four key areas in the marketing mix (known as the 4Ps) on which a business person can focus:

- The product
- The place
- The price
- The promotion.

The product

This needs to attain a consistent standard of quality. For example, Burger King, Pizza Hut and other franchise operators focus on ensuring that the quality of their products is consistent. Customers need predictability much more than surprises. For smaller firms, too, this is an important area – how to deliver a product of quality on a consistent basis. Often, due to staff shortages, financial constraints, time management or other reasons the focus on product quality can be lost.

Everything must be done to ensure consistency of quality and by doing this it will actually be possible to put in systems and procedures which lower costs or at least get them under control. For example, a picture framing business priced its products on a cost plus basis but on checking the detail found they were using the

wrong cost base and varying the source of cost informati
to job.

By bringing a sense of order into the way the product or serv
provided, making quality consistent and consolidating the costin
system, there is a perceived value added in the eyes of the
customers. They feel more comfortable about the source of supply
and perhaps become more loyal.

Place of business/distribution

The loyalty which beings to build up with existing clients through
existing products may need further reinforcing by attending to
distribution issues.

Efficiency and customer service

Products need to move to clients quickly, predictably, without fuss
so that costs can be held down. From the time the client places an
order to its delivery there needs to be an efficient process which can
be relied on.

The supplier, therefore, needs to ask himself questions such as,
'Are we meeting customers' expectations in areas they consider
important?' Figure 2.16 provides an example of a situation where
the business evaluates its performance against that of a competitor.
In this example, our company performs better only on these factors
which are less important to the customer! Some urgent action is
needed.

Cost focus

The drive for efficiency means a focus on forcing total costs down in
the long term. For example, to ensure that products reach customers
in good condition, thereby reducing claims for damage, it may be
necessary to increase the cost of packaging and method of delivery.
The focus on cost is therefore related to the whole transaction not
just to elements of it.

For example, there was a time when soft fruits were shipped in
refrigerated containers from Sri Lanka. When the exporter
switched to air freight, the unit cost of freight increased but losses
were reduced, lowering the total cost. In addition, with the fruit
arriving in prime condition, sales and volume demand increased,
accelerating the cash flow.

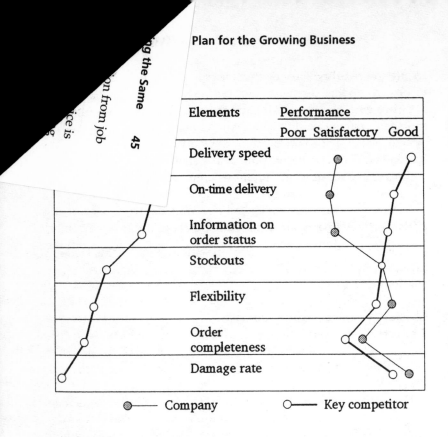

Figure 2.16 *Customer service analysis*

There are often several trade-offs with a focus on cost, the key issue being that the business person should consider all the issues. If the business is successful in reducing costs, this provides a margin of safety and increased profitability which makes staying much the same worth while. There is no need to pass on cost reductions unless competitive pressure increases.

Loyalty

One of the main threats to a business which has decided to stay much the same is competition. Because it has no plans to move in any other business direction, it just cannot afford to lose customers. Therefore, the businessman needs to consider ways of generating loyalty apart from ensuring consistent quality. The two main opportunities are to 'delight' customers often enough to keep them interested and to try to 'lock' them in.

- To delight them, pay that little extra attention to detail, make it fun to do business with your business. Send the goods on time, pack them more attractively, remember the customers' names or their preferences.
- To lock in a customer it is necessary to focus on part of the transaction. For example, a wholesaler of flowers obtained the keys to his retail customers' premises and not only delivered the flowers, but also arranged them. He did this over a Sunday evening so that the florists had no additional work on Mondays when they opened up. A tool-hire business issued 'membership' cards to customers which entitled them to special terms and thus encouraged repeat business.

In some companies it is possible to link clients' computers with those of the supplier to increase the flow of information, deal with order processing and so on. Similarly, some supplier/client relationships can be locked together through the supply of tools, components, technology or other relationships. Care needs to be taken that the locking-in process is mutually beneficial and that complacency does not set it.

Pricing

In many situations, loyal customers are less price sensitive because they value the relationship for several other reasons, some of which have already been covered. If competitive activity is not fierce, it should be possible to establish a profitable price level which allows the business to provide that extra added value. Earlier, it was suggested that there needs to be a focus on costs, especially through making consistent products and ensuring efficient distribution. If the business is successful in driving down costs, it will achieve an increased profit margin if prices to customers are held constant. However, increasing the perceived added value, delighting the customers and finding a way to lock them in will enable an increase in prices to be made at little additional cost.

Promotion

The issue of customer loyalty and therefore retention cannot be over-emphasized when the strategic option is to remain much the same. Therefore, the final element of the marketing mix – promotion

– is a focus on building and managing relationships. This goes beyond the service delivery described earlier and should build on the concepts suggested, such as the relationship life cycle and the Johari Window (see page 32).

In addition, the building and managing of relationships will require additional competencies in the areas of negotiation, communication and the more general point about building trust and dealing with people. All of these issues are outside the scope of this book, but suffice it to say that they are central to the human side of marketing.

APPLICATION ACTIVITIES

1. Analyse your existing customers in terms of the following:
    (a) Sales trends
    (b) Sales of particular products
    (c) Quality of relationships you have with them
    (d) Their profitability to your business.

2. Ask *why* the sales trends, sales of products and the quality of the relationships are what they are. Take the 'why' analysis deep enough to get to grips with real issues (see the 'why' diagram on page 192).

3. Analyse your existing products/services in terms of the following:
    (a) Sales trends
    (b) Which customers buy the most of the products
    (c) Are the products technically up-to-date and provide a high level of quality?
    (d) Do they make a positive contribution to profitability?

4. Identify why particular products sell where they do and whether you can sell more to the same clients. The gaps you identify with analysis of *'why'* will help to develop an action plan.

5. Check the implications of the activities on your finance and people in Chapters 6 and 7.

SUMMARY

Whether or not the company is on this part of the business directions map by chance or by choice, it does offer the business person some distinct advantages. These stem mainly from the fact that risks are minimized because there are so many 'knowns' within the business environment. Having said that, the future of the company is held hostage to:

(a) the stability and continuing success of its customers
(b) the longer-term viability of its products or services
(c) its ability to maintain good relationships with its key customers.

Using the 80/20 rule it is possible to identify the few customers with whom ongoing business will be critical to the future success of the enterprise. With these customers it is important to identify what constitutes the decision-making unit and to influence all its members. Relationship building, both at a company and individual level, was shown to rely on the skills of getting feedback and also of disclosure.

The product or service has to be looked at in a new way, as a core with a surround. Seen in this light, customers buy a whole package and often items in the product surround can have more bearing on the sale than the functional performance of the product or service itself.

Another issue concerning the product or service was its position in its life cycle. Although sometimes difficult to draw it was nevertheless a useful means of analysis and helped to identify some important strategic issues. Above all else, the product or service provides the means by which the company locks in its customers and provides a 'strategic fit'.

Finally, the critical success factors were considered for a company which pursues the strategic option of supplying existing customers with existing products or services. These were how the company promoted itself, how it managed its product/service package to extract the greatest margins consistent with the customer satisfaction provided, how customer service had to enhance the relationship between the company and its customers and how costs must be minimized.

Unlike other strategic options where there has to be investment in finding new customers or new products, this part of the business options map does offer genuine possibilities for minimizing costs.

3

Profiting from New Products and Services: Selling New Products to Existing Customers

INTRODUCTION

The company which wants to profit from new products and services, by selling them to existing customers, has to view this strategy more as a form of expanding business relationships than just selling new products. This approach to expansion will cause the company to ask more of the right questions in order to increase profits.

As with all the other possible business directions, adopting this one brings with it some distinct advantages but there are also some drawbacks. It is the way in which these 'pluses' are balanced against the 'minuses' which ultimately determines how successful the business will be. However, before examining these forces in more detail it helps to understand some of the reasons which might push a company in this particular business direction. Here are just some of them:

- Existing products or services have become tired and dated, or overtaken by new technology.
- Demand for existing products is falling.

- The company finds it easier to develop new products or services than to find new customers.
- Existing customers are mainly large and growing.
- Existing customers believe in the company's ability to deliver, based on past performance.
- The company has a high level of understanding about how its customers' requirements are changing.
- The company's customers are, on the whole, innovators themselves.

Factors such as these can create a powerful undertow which can sweep the company along, regardless of how it might wish to determine its own future. Yet to be drawn along in this way is not necessarily bad; the danger only arises when the company feels that everything is getting out of control and it is being manipulated by its surrounding circumstances. In other words, whose hand is on the tiller of change?

THE BENEFITS OF BEING IN THIS SECTOR OF THE BUSINESS DIRECTIONS MAP

The positive outcomes of being in this position of the map can include:

- Building on existing relationships, where trust has formed and clients are prepared to expand the nature of the business relationship.
- It is often far more cost effective to increase the volume of business with existing clients than it is to try to win new customers.
- The growing relationship with the client brings other people into the 'network', so spreading the risks, in case the key contact moves on for some reason.
- The growing network may provide new opportunities with existing clients or with their referrals.
- The company is forced into developing a more up-to-date product portfolio.
- The innovative response to existing customer needs cements the relationship between the customer and the company, thereby making it more difficult for competitors to intervene.
- The company can increase its margins by exploiting the innovative 'added value'.

- The innovative posture of the company helps to create a positive identity for the organization, which in turn can be motivational for those within it.
- New products and services can create options for exploiting new markets.

Attractive though these are, there are also some potential pitfalls.

Disadvantages

- The success rate of new products and services is notoriously poor.
- The company may be driven to develop new outputs before it has been able to exploit its earlier ones fully, ie they were nowhere near the end of their life cycle.
- The company can be trapped into developing new products or services for which there is little total demand.
- The company may become insidiously drawn into such specialized areas that it becomes totally dependent upon the whims of a few key customers.
- The company may not be able to maintain the innovative drive and flexibility to remain successful in this business arena.

All these factors have a very strong possibility of driving up costs or reducing revenue, both of which can be a death knell to the growing business. However, the scale of the benefits or the disadvantages to a large extent depends upon how 'new' products and services are defined.

HOW NEW IS NEW?

As was shown in Chapter 1 the idea of 'newness' can range from a minor modification to the original product or service, to a new and revolutionary concept altogether. While it was convenient from the point of view of the business directions map to show this range of possibilities as a straight-line continuum, it can often be more creative to view it as shown in Figure 3.1.

Whether or not the sources of innovation are juxtaposed as shown in Figure 3.1 is of little consequence. What should be recognized is that each of these sources can be equally valid in terms of generating

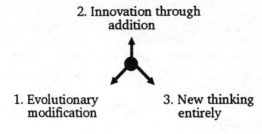

Figure 3.1 *Sources of innovation*

new products or services. What is equally clear is that in terms of risks and costs, these sources could be viewed in this order:

1. Evolutionary modification
2. Innovation through addition
3. New thinking.

Here, 3 represents the most radical and hence a risky departure from current practice.

Not surprisingly, as will be shown, each of these sources of innovation requires different management. Moreover, they rely on different tools or techniques which can help to produce results.

Exercise 3.1	'Me too' products and services

Some businesses, no matter how they try, seem to be stuck with standard products or services, for example, they might make electrical plugs, plastic tubing, envelopes and so on. Often price appears to be the only strategic weapon available to them. However, there are winners in price wars and smaller companies in particular are vulnerable because they have fewer resources to sustain the campaign over a long period.

Therefore, it can be important to try to look at the product or market in a broader, more creative way, as this checklist suggests:

1. Is the product/service really non-differentiated, ie incapable of being separated from competitors' offers?

2. Could an improvement in product quality or design merit a price increase?
3. Are there any significant cost or other benefits for the customer using the product/service?
4. Have these benefits been promoted and exploited?
5. If more was known about customers, could it reveal new benefits which could be exploited?
6. Can anything be done to alter the company image, rather than the product?
7. Can the overall marketing approach be changed, for example telephone sales rather than direct selling, change advertising etc?
8. Can improved delivery methods be developed which would differentiate the product from its competitors, for example, batchsize, easier ordering, time of day etc?
9. Can guarantees be made more attractive to customers, for example, extended period of cover?
10. Can the product be linked to another or be made part of a total package?
11. Can alternative uses be developed for the product?
12. Would making the product larger, smaller or in other materials create a differential advantage?
13. Can additional services be added to the product, for example, maintenance, training, financing etc?
14. If the product was sold into different markets, would this achieve differentiation, for example, from government to commercial, from industrial to retail, from home markets to export etc?
15. Can the product/service be repackaged in a way to achieve differentiation?
16. Could the product be differentiated by using new distribution channels, for example, sweets sold at garages instead of confectioners, cosmetics sold at home instead of in stores etc?

WHERE DOES THE STIMULUS FOR CHANGE ORIGINATE?

Like all good marketers, most people could respond to this question in a flash. 'From customers' would be the deafening response, and taken at face value they would be right. However, let us test out this hypothesis with a little story.

Let us step back in time to the eighteenth century when the embryonic Royal Mail was showing signs of becoming a growth business. Imagine that we made mail coaches and, being forward looking, decided to do some customer research. No doubt we would talk to drivers and ask them how satisfied they were with our product, and what we might do to make their lot a happier one. A few of the users would tell us that there were some unexplained rattles at particular speeds, or that wheel changes were very difficult to make while on the open road. These would be the very points we could latch on to. From information like this it would be possible to design an improved mail coach.

Other coach drivers might take a different approach. Their life might be made easier if they had better roads and a reduced fear of being stopped by highwaymen. What should we do with this information? Branch out into the construction industry? Provide armed guards? The chances are we would dismiss it out of hand because it appears to have nothing to do with the coach-making business.

There might be other drivers still who were completely fed up with sitting behind smelly horses and getting soaked every time it rained. For them, being on a coach at all was a misery. What they would prefer would be to remain in their cosy office and fax information to its destination. However, these people were clearly mad, because such technology had not been invented yet … but then again, nor had market research.

A silly story? Certainly. Yet it serves to illustrate some important points regarding products and innovation.

First, like the mail coach, a product exists only to solve problems. If the problem disappears, or a better means of solving it comes along, then that product is redundant. This has always been the case and presumably always will be. Seeing itself as being in the 'coach-building business' could obscure what it was the company really offered its customers. Being unclear about its real 'product' meant that it misread the value of market research. Instead of developing tomorrow's problem-solver, the company wasted time and resources titivating yesterday's offering.

This point is well illustrated by a GRP (glass reinforced plastics) company who made small sailing dinghies. When under pressure to develop new products it suddenly recognized that its expertise was not just in boat building, but in making watertight vessels. This revelation led the company to see that if it could keep water out, it could also keep water in. To cut a long story short, these creative insights materialized with the company developing a range of water storage tanks which it sold in vast quantities to the desert regions of the Middle East.

Second, it is clearly a myth that innovation is merely a matter of asking people what they want and then making it. While this might work in markets which are stable and essentially customer driven, technological advances are such that yesterday's science fiction becomes today's reality. Thus, a high level of innovation is supply driven and has little to do with customer demand. For example, musical birthday cards exist because manufacturers of microchips were desperate to find an outlet for their surplus production, and many computer technology applications are being developed in advance of customer demand.

Akin to this issue is the fact that the company might not have the resources or expertise available to move to a new level of problem solving. It might be stuck with its current level of technology and have to seek a means of surviving within this context.

The third lesson to come out of the mail coach story is the need to ask the right kinds of question. Those that focus on the efficacy of the current product or service are bound to lead to a 'modification response'. Those that focus on customer requirements are clearly more open ended. They have the potential to uncover wider issues, which in the longer term might provide stronger clues about the nature of the required innovation.

It might be helpful at this point to take a few moments to consider two important questions:

1. Have you asked your existing clients what proportion of their spend on the type of products and services which you supply comes to your business? If it is 100 per cent you are doing very well. However, if you are only getting a small proportion, there might be additional opportunities for your firm.
2. The follow-through question might be to ask if the customer is in a position, or likely, to increase their spend with your business.

There might be other clues from these two questions, especially if linked to data on trends, profitability (see Chapter 6) and quality of relationships.

CREATIVITY AND INNOVATION

Creativity is the process which generates new and unusual ideas. Of themselves, however, ideas achieve very little. Only when they are converted into something with a practical use can innovation be said to have taken place. Thus, creativity is the input and innovation the output. For a company to have one without the other is to be, at best, an also-ran.

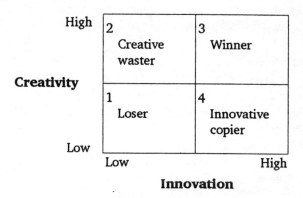

Figure 3.2 *Creativity and innovation*

In Figure 3.2 the relationship between creativity and innovation is considered in more detail. Organizations which are low on both creativity and innovation can only finish up with a range of 'me too' products and services. With nothing to differentiate them from competing offers, such companies are doomed to compete on price alone. This invariably traps then in an ever-accelerating downward spiral, since there is always someone who will charge less.

Those high on creativity but low on innovation are good at generating ideas, but poor at converting them into a saleable product or service. Thus, their output somehow always seems to be 'half-baked' and fails to make the impact the original ideas deserved.

The converse of this, the low creativity, high innovation company, is not good at generating new ideas, but it is likely to be an adept copier.

The winning position arises from a combination of high characteristics in both creativity and innovation.

Creativity in product/service modification

As was shown earlier, this road towards innovation is essentially an evolutionary process where each successive change is a modest improvement. Such changes can certainly be customer driven, but there is also an opportunity to generate improvements by using 'idea-generating' techniques.

Three which are relatively simple to use are:

- competitive analysis
- attribute listing
- turning objections into positives.

Competitive analysis

This operates as follows. Let us, for example, consider two fast-food restaurants. The first step is to identify the **critical success factors** from the customer's viewpoint. These are listed in Table 3.1. Note that, because we are focusing on critical factors, there should never be more than three or four.

Table 3.1   Example of competitive analysis

Critical success factors	Our company (Score out of 10)	Competitor (Score out of 10)
Quality of food	7	9
Cleanliness	8	6
Waiting time	5	5
Friendliness	8	5

The two companies are then assessed against these factors by some form of scoring (here it is marks out of 10). What this indicates is that 'our company's' business could be considerably enhanced if the quality of the food was improved, at least to match that of the competitor. Also, an advantage would be gained if slicker service could be provided to reduce waiting time.

On the other two factors, cleanliness and friendliness, our company outscores the competitor. Even so, it would be dangerous to become complacent about these. Thus, it would be important to ensure that there was no back-sliding with regard to current standards.

From this relatively simple technique it can be seen how an

existing service or product can be modified to get closer to customer expectations. Using this approach ensures that any investment which is made in the 'new product' or service will be guaranteed to improve its acceptability and competitive positioning.

Attribute listing

This is a 'supply-side' improvement approach. It operates like this. Imagine that the company produced a traditional hammer. See Figure 3.3.

Key attributes

1. Wooden handle
2. Metal head
3. Fixing of head to handle

Figure 3.3 *Attribute listing (an example)*

The key attributes of the product (in this case, although the technique works just as well for a service) would be listed as shown in Figure 3.3. Each would then be analysed in turn and a number of alternatives considered. So, for example, in place of the wooden handle it might be possible to have:

- different material, such as steel, carbon fibre etc.
- different length of handle for appearance and mechanical advantage.
- a handgrip provided, for example, plastic/rubber to absorb shock and reduce danger of losing grip.
- a loop or clip could be provided to make it easier to store or attach to belt while not in use.
- it could be coloured so that it would be easy to identify on a cluttered work bench.
- the head could be similarly considered from the point of view of size, shape, material, and perhaps even the prospect of multiple, interchangeable heads. Finally, the method of fixing the handle to the head would be subjected to the same process.

From this welter of alternatives, a new hammer could be designed with distinct advantages over its predecessor in terms of appearance, performance and safety. Clearly the Mark 2 hammer would justify a higher price than the original 'me too' implement.

Again, this is a somewhat simplistic example chosen to illustrate a point. However, if something as simple as a three-part tool can yield such a high level of creative potential, just think what the options must be for more complex products or services.

Turning objections into positives

In the course of dealing with customers it might be discovered that certain objections keep cropping up about the product or service. For example:

'The handles are too small to be comfortable.'
'The pack size is not really large enough.'
'It's really too complicated for our staff to understand.'

Whatever the complaints, if they are genuine and unbiased, they provide the supplier with free advice about how to make his or her output more attractive to customers. In this way, a 'new' and 'improved' version is born.

Creativity from adding to the product or service

Many innovations are not in themselves new but arise from using existing products or services in an unusual combination, or finding a use for them in a different environment. Thus, a home delivery pizza service is nothing more than a combination of a take-away food service and the postman. Similarly, the only new feature of in-car radios and music players is that technology enabled units to be miniaturized and to run off a low voltage supply. The equipment already existed for use in a domestic environment.

There is, therefore, considerable creative scope to find 'new' products or services by:

- making existing products larger or smaller
- making them suitable for use in different environments
- providing them in different colours or packaging
- combining the features of two products into one new benefit
- providing them with 'bolt-on extras'.

This last approach has been exploited with considerable success by the manufacturers of the 'Cindy' type of dolls for girls, or 'Action Man' for boys. With these the basic figure comes relatively cheaply, but the various changes of costume and their goods and chattels are all available ... at a price. Since it seems that no self-respecting doll can live without all the trappings of a film star life-style, the profit potential for these 'new' products has been tremendous.

In terms of idea-generating techniques, innovations of this nature lend themselves to matrix or cube approaches. The fundamental concept behind idea generation is that many ideas will be stupid or unsuitable, therefore it is important to produce a large number of ideas in order to arrive at the rare gem. Each of the approaches which follows has the merit of using each new factor as a multiplier, thereby creating a large number of options in a short space of time.

Matrix Approach

This could have been used by the GRP company mentioned above. It could have constructed a matrix of possibilities for making containers as shown in Figure 3.4.

In the time it took to construct this matrix (approximately one minute) 63 ideas (7 × 9) have been generated. That is to say, each

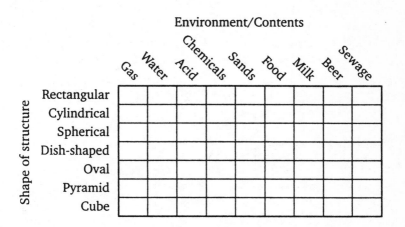

Figure 3.4 *The ideas matrix*

combination has a product potential. Each new item on the top line adds another seven potential ideas, while each new item on the side adds a further nine. The trick is to identify dimensions for the matrix which have meaning. For a company making containers 'environment/contents' and 'shape' might be reasonable dimensions. For a company making pet food, 'flavour' and 'can size' could be more pertinent. Even a film maker could use this approach, for example, 'type of film', for example musical, costume drama, thriller, war, western; and 'setting', for example modern, last century, America, Europe, city, country. The matrix can in turn be multiplied if a new dimension is added, thus making it a cube.

The ideas cube

This approach can generate a high number of potential product ideas in a relatively short time. For example, the original matrix in Figure 3.4 which provided 63 ideas can be upgraded to yield 378 (63×6) by adding a further dimension, surface finish, see Figure 3.5. Moreover, each new factor on this third dimension automatically adds another 63 possibilities to the ideas bank.

. On pure statistical chance, there should be at least two or three ideas within the 378 which will convert into winning products. With such a prolific idea-generating technique, the greater problem becomes that of evaluating them.

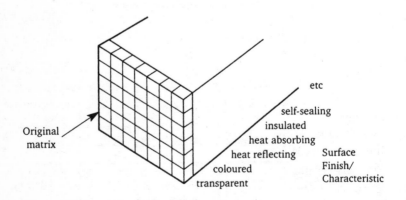

Figure 3.5   *The ideas cube*

Evaluation of ideas

Not only is the challenge to find the best dimensions for the matrix or cube in itself creative, but also there is the problem of choosing the best options from such a large number of starters.

Unfortunately, there can be no hard and fast rules laid down for evaluation, except that as a process it generally works better if the emphasis is on rejecting 'no-hope' ideas, rather than picking winners. With this in mind, the company should consider the criteria to which a good idea would be matched, then use these to sieve all the ideas in the bank. For example, a promising idea might have to meet these criteria:

- Be technically feasible for the company
- Be compatible with existing work
- Be compatible with the resources at our disposal.

The technically feasible sieve will eliminate a number of possible ideas straight away. The subsequent sieves will, as like as not, reduce the original welter of ideas into a shortlist. At this stage a new set of criteria will need to be established, for example:

- Will the idea appeal to existing customers?
- Is there much competition?
- Will it provide a high margin?

This second level of evaluation needs to be conducted in more detail and might require some research to find the answers. This is why it is important only to address these questions to a selected group of ideas with potential, rather than every idea generated. Ideas which survive this rigorous examination are clearly those with very high potential.

From this brief description about idea evaluation, it should be apparent that no two companies will necessarily use the same judging criteria. One might be interested in volume sales, whereas another will be capacity limited. One might be seeking to exploit new technology, while another will wish to remain with the familiar. What is important is that the selected idea is matched as well as possible to the company's circumstances and ambitions. If even the best idea is ill-matched, it would be better to leave it alone and instead try to generate another bank of possibilities.

New thinking entirely

The guru of so-called lateral thinking, Edward de Bono, claims that the reason it is so difficult to come up with genuinely new ideas is that people develop a 'mind set' and are conditioned by their existing circumstances. He likens it to a person searching for buried treasure. Having spent time and trouble digging a hole, the searcher is reluctant to abandon it. Rather than start again elsewhere, he decides to dig just a little bit deeper, or make the hole wider. In thinking terms, that person is merely toying with the original concept. A radical idea will only come about from 'digging a new hole' somewhere else.

This analogy is certain supported by breakthroughs in scientific thinking. Whether the current concept was that the world was flat or the Earth was at the centre of the solar system, eventually evidence piled up to prove that the fundamental belief was itself untrue. Once scientists were released from these earlier 'holes', new ways of thinking led to many new discoveries. Thus, the evolution of scientific discovery is characterized by bursts of inventiveness which accompany a genuine breakthrough, one which proved that earlier thinking was far from being the truth.

Thus, lateral thinking means looking at things differently and not being trapped by old thinking. A good example of this in action was the 'invention' of Clingfilm. Plastic film is produced by forming the semi-molten material first into a tube, then this is inflated to become a bubble. The thickness of the film is determined by the diameter of the bubble. On a continuous process, the plastic sets and the air bubble is then slit, leaving the film to be wound on to large rollers.

The bugbear of the process technician was that in its manufacture the film became electrostatically charged, which made it difficult to manipulate since it had a tendency to stick to anything with which it came into contact. Much effort and ingenuity went into solving this production problem, for it was the source of considerable wastage. Then one day someone asked the seemingly stupid question if any use could be made of the reject material. From being a process problem, Clingfilm became a product in its own right.

This turning of the original problem on its head is similar to the boat builders mentioned earlier who realized that if they could keep water out of a vessel, they could just as easily keep it in one.

It is not easy to identify idea-generating techniques which produce radical thinking like this. These incidents are often the outcome of a sudden shaft of insight. Indeed, research suggests that certain personality types are more inclined to come up with more original ideas than others. The problem is that these 'creative' people cannot be creative all the time while, paradoxically, at critical moments, 'non-creative' people can deliver whatever is required.

This book is not the place to go more deeply into this fascinating conundrum, except to say that creative ideas are generally more forthcoming under the following circumstances:

- When people are encouraged to think they are creative
- When people are relaxed, even day-dreaming
- When people are having fun in informal surroundings
- When anarchic thought is encouraged.

Not surprisingly, Archimedes leapt from the bath with his great discovery, not the boardroom.

Brainstorming

Probably the technique most compatible with the conditions listed above is brainstorming. This operates on three main premisses:

1. The collective brain-power of a group can outperform any individual when it comes to ideas.
2. People can be more creative if they suspend judgement on their ideas, in other words express them without censorship.
3. It is important to develop quantity because this increases the odds on uncovering a winning idea.

Most people will have heard of, or experienced, this technique. It operates best with about eight people who are encouraged to call out whatever ideas occur to them, and without comment these are listed so that all the group can see them. In this way the ideas which are generated can stimulate new ones. Only when a number of ideas are assembled should any attempt be made to evaluate them.

Simple though this is, many who try the process come nowhere near the target which is claimed for an experienced group: 150 ideas in 20 minutes. Among the reasons for falling short of this will be:

- People still censor their own ideas and do not voice them – regardless of what is said
- Someone dominates the session
- The group is unfamiliar with working together
- There was no warm-up session.

This last point is particularly important. Just as a top-flight athlete would warm up before a race, or a top golfer will hit many practice balls before teeing off, so should a brainstorming group limber up before tackling its real task.

The warm-up should last for about 20 minutes, and should challenge the group to come up with as many uses as they can find for some everyday object, such as a safety pin, matchstick, paper clip, or the like. At the end of the warm-up, the group should review what helped or hindered its productivity, if necessary having another dummy run to put these things right. Only then, perhaps after a short break, should it proceed on to its major task.

An important consideration at this point is that if an idea has resulted in a totally new product, it is well worth finding out about the patenting process. For a nominal fee it is possible to register the patent for a year while investigations about the technical and market feasibility are carried out. If the product appears to hold its initial level of promise, full patent applications can be put in. It is best to seek the advice of a patent agent or to approach the Patent Office direct.

By protecting the product it is possible to exploit the potential fully in the market place.

Finding and buying ideas and products

From the foregoing section it can be seen that, while creativity can be fun, it can also be time-consuming and perhaps lead the company into areas where deep down it would prefer not to go. Therefore, as an alternative to the company tacitly setting out to do everything itself, when faced with an option to provide a new product or service, it could look further afield. The main possibilities which spring to mind are:

1. It could buy the new product and sell it on.
2. It could enter into a strategic alliance with another company on the basis of some form of reciprocal trading, for example they both agree to sell the other's products or services.
3. It could scan data banks of products (such as the Patent Office) for new ideas.
4. It could license in a new product to fit in with others offered to existing customers.
5. Repackaging the benefits.
6. Modifications.

Many companies use these approaches to good effect once they can be sure that the quality standards will meet customer requirements, and that the financial arrangements allow for suitable margins to be built in.

1. Buying in a product or service This is perhaps the simplest solution to describe. It requires the company to scan trade directories or pick up ideas from contacts or exhibitions. It can then decide on a deal with another firm which has a product or service to complement the ones it is already offering. There will be a need to provide full technical back-up for the new product and suitable assessment must be carried out to establish how compatible it is with the direction of the business, the other products or services, and the ability of the sales and service people. The margins should also be attractive to make it all worthwhile.

Different forms of contract can be agreed with the new supplier. For example, either a straight purchase and resale or some form of percentage as a sales commission are two possibilities. The terms and conditions will depend upon a number of factors such as:

1. the size of the supplying company
2. its usual contractual arrangements
3. its business objectives
4. the amount of work the company has to put into the bought-in products, such as repackaging or providing instructions in the correct language.

2. A strategic alliance or reciprocal trading It is possible that two firms require each other's products to complement their own. In this case each firm can sell to the other on preferential terms and thus be able to offer a better package of benefits to their own customers. For example, a firm which makes spiral staircases might decide to create an alliance with a firm which makes straight stairs so that both have the capacity to sell a more complete range of products. They do need to be separated geographically or be selling into different market segments so that they do not compete head on.

3. Scanning data banks There are many sources of new ideas and products. Visits to exhibitions, reading the right journals, and talking to potential users are some methods available to small firms. Perhaps the most extensive and least used source of product innovation is the data stored at the Patent Office. For a nominal fee it is possible to search the data on products which have been patented. One does have to be focused on the product category, but with appropriate key words and search methods it should be possible to arrive at a short list of products which might be explored. In the first instance it may be possible to find products which are not being effectively marketed, so an approach to the person holding the patent with an offer to market the product to your customers might bring mutual benefit.

4. License in   There are other possibilities to take on a licence to make and sell products which have been patented. Perhaps the best-known examples are the 'workmate' which has been licensed to Black & Decker to manufacture and sell, and the Dolby sound system which the inventor decided to license to as many electronics firms as possible. The terms of the licence provide extensive royalties and a consultancy contract enabling the inventor to advise and invent improvements with clients. From the clients' perspective this is an added bonus as they have a highly talented inventor available to them to improve the product constantly.

5. Repackaging the benefits   The existing products may serve a certain range of decision-makers among your existing customers. By redefining the benefits of the products or services it may be possible to appeal to a larger constituency and hence increase the sales of products and services with the existing pool of customers. For instance, the yellow Post-it notes from 3M appeal to a wide range of customers. However, by offering to print messages on to the Post-its (with cartoons) it is possible to extend sales to existing customers.

The same technology has been applied to flip-chart paper, so trainers who wish to stick course ideas on to the walls of hotel rooms while conducting training no longer have to go in search of sticky tape, Blue-Tack or drawing pins.

Certain firms attempt to delight the customers by slight modification to their offering, such as a consultant who delivered client reports which included their logo on the cover.

6. Modifications   Perhaps the most familiar area of innovation comes from modification and improvement after the initial breakthrough has been made with a product. The most common examples are the improvements to computer software, which arrive in the market place with amazing frequency. Other modifications to products might enable other departments to purchase. However, product modifications may have to be linked to other research and development activity.

Research and development

This is clearly not available to all firms as an option. However, firms which are technically based may have to allocate a proportion of their resources to constant development of new ideas and opportunities. For small businesses, the key decision to be made by the owners is whether this is what drives them, assuming the originators of the business are also the technical entrepreneurs. Often scientists have great difficulty in adjusting to life as a business person and would rather continue as a scientist. Whatever the tension is in terms of desires and competence, a decision will have to be made, as the research and development aspect of a technical firm is also the lifeblood of future opportunities. However, sufficient energy and resources also have to be put into ensuring that existing products and services are not neglected.

The concept of adding value

As was said earlier, if the product or service is at heart merely a problem-solver then any replacement for it must, by definition, be a better problem-solver. This means that the new offer must act faster, be safer, be more reliable, be more efficient, or whatever. If it cannot show these added benefits then it begs the question, 'Why develop it in the first place?'

Another reason for providing added value is that it enables the company to charge more for its new product or service. However, the customer will only be prepared to pay for this if the benefit the new offer bestows is what he or she seeks. As ever in marketing, the answer lies in knowing one's customers as much as possible, and being clear about what they seek from the transaction. If this information is not known, it will be important to find out.

One could ask customers if they would be prepared to pay extra for specific improvements in the product or service. The drawback with this approach is that the psychology is all wrong, for very few people want to pay more for anything.

Therefore, a different approach would be to describe the new improved product or service and to stress its several benefits. Then the customer would be asked if, in the interests of keeping prices down, some of these had to be omitted, which could he or she do without. With such a process of elimination, naturally enough, only the high-value benefits remain. It is on the basis of providing these that the supplier can set new prices and increase margins.

CRITICAL SUCCESS FACTORS ASSOCIATED WITH THIS BUSINESS DIRECTION

The nature of the new product or service is at the heart of the new products to existing customers area of the business map. It was for this reason that the bulk of this chapter has focused on it. Nevertheless, there are still some other critical factors which need to be considered.

Price

The key issue facing a business is about matching the price to a number of factors.

Objectives

For example, is the company trying to add value to the relationship? Hang on to an existing client against stiff competition? Reposition the company in some way?

To make a correct decision a considerable amount of good quality information will be required. The questions which might be asked at this point are:

- Do you know how much profit you make from each customer?
- Do your customers pay promptly?
- Does your customer list include those who might be considered 'blue-chip'?
- What is the potential level of business you can do with each customer (are you doing this much of it already)?
- Do you know what it costs to service each customer?
- What are the cost structures for each product or service?
- What is the price level of your main competition and how do you compare?

New costs

New costs may be associated with extending your products or services to existing clients. For example, there may be a need to recruit new staff or move premises; additional investment may be required for machinery or larger marketing costs might have to be incurred. Therefore, the prices you charge will have to be capable of recovering the additional new costs over a given time frame.

Cash flow

When expansion occurs one of the key decisions is how soon will cash flow cover the outgoings incurred on expansion plans. It will be useful to carry out a cash flow forecast in some detail (see Chapter 6) before committing to expansion.

The effect on prices will be that a higher price (which may result in lower volume but not always) may help to recover costs sooner. A lower price with lower margins may help with sales but could create cash-flow problems. It is extremely helpful to try out three 'what-if' calculations, based on pessimistic and optimistic views of the market and one between the two extremes. This 'sensitivity analysis' can highlight where problems might occur and allow you to look at relationships between income and costs in more detail.

Service and follow-up

Launching a new product (or a modified one) to existing customers has the distinct cost advantages of low marketing effort. However, new products are also associated with new learning in terms of the back-up which has to be offered. These must be taken into account when setting the price. Perhaps the key advantage which a company has is that existing clients are not often too fussed about prices from existing suppliers, as they have developed a relationship and trust in the service (reliability, peace of mind etc). Therefore, when a new service is offered with added value it should be possible to seek a higher price which reflects that improvement.

Promotion

When considering promotion of the new product or service to existing customers, one is building on a strength: the relationship which already exists. Thus, the 'entry' costs and effort will be lower than those for potential new customers. The four essential steps in trying to promote the sale of new products to existing customers are as follows:

- Increase the amount of networking which is carried out with existing clients. Establish who the important contacts are and what their role is in the buying cycle. For example, are they important in establishing the need for new products, do they influence the choice of supplier, can they determine cost levels and who actually places the order and is responsible for ensuring payment?
- This first stage is akin to market research. It is an important first step as it will help to pitch the marketing message more effectively by 'tuning' the benefits offered to each player in the decision-making unit. For example, to offer the best prices for adhesive plaster to a surgeon whose main preoccupation is with the effectiveness of the plaster would be a waste of time. Yet for the buyer, to focus on reliability of delivery and cost-effectiveness would be right. Similarly, if the nurse has a role to play in the decision, the benefit sought might be ease of application and wound management.
- Once the decision-making unit has been properly assessed, the firm should then develop its marketing message according to the needs of the target audience and begin to raise awareness of its new product and indeed itself (if new contacts are involved). To be trusted as a current supplier may be a great asset and help to open doors to new contacts within existing client firms.

Raising awareness of new products to existing clients cannot be over-emphasized. One firm had two data bases, one 'upstairs' in accounts and called the sales ledger, and one downstairs and called 'new prospects list'. The marketing effort was entirely focused on printing glossy literature and sending out vast quantities of brochures to potential new customers, with a relatively small take-up of information. To the audience receiving the glossy literature it was just 'junk mail'. When this firm had a flash of insight and organized a mailing of new products to the clients on its 'sales ledger list' the impact was immediate: sales went up by 30 per cent within three months.

The main reason is that the glossy literature was not 'junk mail', and it was information for existing clients. Of course, the product and prices were also appropriate to client needs.

- To carry out all the above steps the critical additional element is that the firm should provide a budget. Nothing comes free! If there is one area in which most firms fall down it is that marketing plans (especially promotional plans) are not always backed up by an appropriate budget. There are many examples of wasteful spending, such as ad hoc advertising in newspapers (to take advantage of a special offer), mistimed mail shots, over-ambitious glossy literature which fails to carry a useful message, and so on.

A more carefully considered promotional plan should make it possible to assess the cost implications within any given financial year. With this information the entrepreneur can calculate the additional sales required to break even on the new cost level. If the sums add up, the budget should be implemented and built into cash-flow projections (see Chapter 6).

Distribution

The logistics of supplying the new product or service must be calculated and built into the cost structure. For example, is new bulk packaging required? Are new ordering procedures necessary? What will be the inventory levels? How will customer service be managed? And so on.

The more the new product or service departs from its predecessor, the more thought must be given to details of this nature. There are six key issues to be considered when making decisions about delivering the products or services:

- The appropriateness of the channel must be considered. The new product may demand more from the supplier if it is being positioned as a more expensive product or service. Thus, the use of agents or distributors may be affected. Indeed, if the new product competes with an existing source, it may be necessary to offer something more attractive in the way the product is delivered, stored, packaged etc.
- Since the main thrust of selling new products to existing customers is to build on a relationship, it should be possible to find out what the most effective routes are. There should be distinct advantages to both the customer and your company if it is possible.

- It may be necessary to be selective at first, especially if the product is new and there may be teething problems with it. Perhaps you should try it with 'friendly' clients who will be prepared to provide you with constructive advice. Try not to offer a new product to your most important customers first, unless the relationship is so good that they should be the first to receive it.

  Indeed, the need for selectivity may extend to geographic considerations or even restrictions to certain industry sectors. The channels you choose, especially if intermediaries (such as agents) are used, must be able to cope with the new product in all its forms and potential future growth.

- The main message which is being offered by the three points above is that considerable ambiguity might exist when choosing distribution channels for the new product. Therefore, be prepared to scan a number of options and try to consider those few that appear to be the most viable, before selecting just one main channel.

- Although channels of distribution are thought to be important for the flow of goods, the less acknowledged role is to help pass information back from the customer. For example, mail order firms are in almost direct contact (if somewhat impersonally) whereas firms selling to agents who then sell to wholesalers and then to retailers before reaching the customer have the double disadvantage of not being in contact with the end user of the product and being dependent on the retailer for the image of his or her product and company.

  Decisions about channels will affect the level of information flowing from customers and this may have to be taken into account.

- With increasing emphasis on customer service, more people are expecting higher standards of reliability from their suppliers. An increasing number of firms are holding less in stock than they used to, because greater reliability of supply is expected and being provided.

The entrepreneur takes a great gamble between launching a product before all the bugs have been removed and waiting to launch a perfect product, only to find that competition has moved in first. A trade-off may be needed between achieving high levels of reliability both of the product and the channel being selected and risking the loss of market share.

STRATEGIC FIT

When a new product is being developed, it is necessary to ask if it fits with how the rest of the products are sold and serviced. For example, a company which marketed industrial Vee belts (fan belts) began to try to sell the pulleys by buying them in from a highly competitive source. In theory this was a good move as it provided a more complete service and increased volume sales to clients. However, the range of pulleys was not wide enough and the firm did not have adequate storage facilities, technical back-up, or trained sales staff in the office familiar with pulleys. In addition, it was in a relatively weak competitive position in the market place since its reputation was earned from belts.

Customers who tried to buy the belts and pulleys from this company found their discounts reduced from the competitor on their other purchases (such as motors, gearboxes etc). Gradually it was realized by the company and its customers that the relationship had to focus on belts where the quality and reliability were high.

APPLICATION ACTIVITIES

1. Clearly identify new products and services in terms of the benefits as well as features.
2. Carry out a gap analysis of your existing customers to identify which ones are most likely to be receptive to new products from you.
3. Consider the detailed cost and human resource implications shown in Chapters 6 and 7 and draft the action points in Chapter 8.
4. Finally, this chapter is rich with action points and if this is the chosen strategy – *set it in motion NOW!*

SUMMARY

The business direction of providing new products for existing customers brings with it a number of advantages. These are mainly concerned with the benefits of renewing the firm's output portfolio and locking it ever closer to its customers. However, as we saw, there are attendant dangers which can stem from being exploited by customers, and being seduced into highly specialized, cul-de-sacs, which ultimately limit the company's business prospects.

The creative challenge this position poses for the company largely depends upon the degree of 'newness' of the replacement product or service. Sometimes slight modifications are enough to solve customers' problems. At other times something entirely new will be required. Techniques for dealing with various levels of newness were discussed with simple examples provided.

While on the surface it would seem that the driving force for new products or services would come from customers, this was not always the case. There are many occasions when innovation is supply driven. How the company establishes what customers require is largely determined by the quality of the questions it asks them.

To get a winning product or service, when so many new ones fail, entails generating a large number of ideas in the first place, then screening out all but the one or two which have high potential.

An alternative to doing it all was for the company to buy in new products or services and sell them on to its customers. An extension of this strategy would be for the company to enter into a reciprocal trading alliance with another supplier.

To safeguard its new ideas the company is advised to consider licensing or patent agreements, which in turn could prove to be saleable assets at some future date.

Finally, we saw that while the new product or service was a dominant issue, its pricing, promotion and distribution also needed to be taken into account. Innovation in these areas could also pay handsome dividends.

4

Finding New Customers for Existing Products

INTRODUCTION

For you to be reading this chapter, the earlier stock-taking exercise, particularly the Strategic Options Questionnaire (see pages 12–14), should have indicated that finding new customers for existing products is a promising and viable strategy for your company. There are some advantages and disadvantages associated with taking this particular route. These will be discussed later in the chapter because they colour much of the operating policies which are required to be successful in following this strategy option. However, to start off it will be worth while considering if the company finds itself pursing this strategy option as a result of conscious management decision, or was it more to do with external forces guiding the company this way? In other words, did it jump or was it pushed?

ACCIDENT OR DESIGN

In some ways what happened in the past should be a secondary issue to what is going to happen in the future. However, a company's history can never quite be shaken off; it does tend to influence much of the company thinking and behaviour in subtle ways. Thus it is that companies which have 'drifted' into this strategic direction might in fact have a stronger basis for being right than their self-directed contemporaries. The outside world has told them that it is this for which they are best suited. Even so, there will be some companies for which there is no other possible option to take. Therefore, regardless of how they come to be in this part of the business directions map, it is likely that companies sharing this position will exhibit many of the following characteristics:

- Customers cannot/do not make repeat purchases
- Products or services are relatively easy to produce in quantity.
- The products/services are fairly standardized (ie not a great range of variants) and easy to describe
- They are easy to transport or distribute
- The company has 'sales' strengths
- The company has products/services for which there is a high demand
- The company is prepared to spend in order to win new customers
- The products/services offer a range of benefits
- Average order size is relatively low.

ADVANTAGES OF SELLING EXISTING PRODUCTS TO NEW CUSTOMERS

For companies following this strategic option there are several advantages.

Product/Service life is maximized

A famous comedian was quoted as saying that 'There is no such thing as a new joke, there are only people who have never heard it before.' In a similar way the product can go on and on for all the time that there are new people to buy it. In reality this means that the company more then recovers the costs associated with developing the product or service in the first place. Moreover, those who have to supply it become expert over time and can therefore guarantee high quality in a minimal production time, thereby in effect minimizing costs.

Not held hostage

The company which is ever seeking new customers can never become locked in and over-dependent on some of them. Therefore, it can never be held hostage to terms which large customers might dictate as an extended relationship develops.

A way of life

Finding new customers becomes a focal point in everything the company does and thus becomes a way of corporate life which is understood by everybody. It can provide a dynamism which ensures that things never stagnate.

There are no boundaries

In a sense the company is free to travel wherever the prospect of sales may lead it. Thus, it is not limited geographically or by types of industry unless it chooses to be. In practice, the only boundaries will be those imposed by costs and imagination.

Broadening the customer base

It is possible to sell existing products to new customers by defining them as market segments. For example, from selling components to the defence industry or the space programme a company may find other applications, as happened with products like Velcro. Thus, one market segment may protect the company if another one goes down.

DISADVANTAGES

It is an unfortunate fact of life that for every silver lining there is a cloud lurking somewhere. This is equally true for those who follow this strategic option. These disadvantages can be crippling if they are not minimized.

Costs of finding new customers

Depending upon the type of industry, it can be shown that winning business from new customers can cost many times more than that of selling to existing ones. For example, some manufacturers calculate it can cost as much as 17 times more. Less high priced businesses show more modest, but nevertheless important, multipliers in the order of three or four times. There are a number of factors which influence the high costs of winning a new customer:

- advertising and publicity
- meeting and relationship building
- administrative procedures
- checking creditworthiness etc.

These are greatly reduced the second time around.

Where to find new customers?

Unless the company has a unique service or product it is unlikely that customers will come beating a path to its door. Instead, the company must go out to find them. Where they are, and which ones will be best, are two eternal dilemmas facing companies which follow this strategic option.

Organizational myopia

In its restless search for new customers, the company can sometimes become short-sighted and fail to recognize that its existing products and services are reaching the end of their useful life. Its failure to win new orders might not be because of shortcomings in its sales efforts, but because its offerings are no longer fashionable or competitive enough when measures against alternatives available to the customer.

Caught up in the hunt

Some companies have their origins in, and focus on, selling. One has a vision of the hunter enjoying the hunt more than the catch. Such a company may not fully analyse the cost implications of selling, preferring to continue hunting because it is fun, involves company cars, expense accounts and is an activity the people are really good at. Clearly, at the heart of any success with the strategy of selling existing products or services to new customers is the company's ability to identify suitable targets to pursue. Let us look at customers more closely.

WHAT IS A CUSTOMER?

The cynical reader will probably mutter something about the sort of person whom you can never please and who is at the root of 90 per cent of all business problems (if not 100 per cent). Heart-felt though such a description might be, it does not do very much to create a positive analysis, so let us start again.

All customers have at least two points in common:

- a need for a product or service
- the ability to pay for it.

For them to have one of these and not the other is to rule them out.

While there might be a few gullible folk who can be talked into buying something which they do not really need, they are few and far between. It is far sounder for the business person to view the purchasing decision as having an element of rationality. If this were not the case, why is it that so many products and services fail? By putting oneself in the customer's shoes, as it were, it becomes possible for the business person to understand more clearly why customers behave as they do.

Understanding customers

The first thing to understand is that the customer, that is to say the person who actually buys the product or service, is not always the user or consumer of it. So, for example, a craftsman who makes expensive wooden rocking horses would have to understand what gave the product its eye-catching appeal to small children, while at the same time understanding the motivations of the adults who bought it.

For the sake of convenience we will continue to refer to customers throughout this chapter, and indeed the book. It will not dilute any of the principles put forward, except that those with consumers who are separate from customers will need to give slightly more thought to how they apply them.

Pressures on the customer

At the time of considering a purchase, the customer is subject to many types of influence. Some of these are self-generated and internal, such as beliefs, hopes, fears, attitudes, perceptions, self-image and so on. These are some of the characteristics which can determine how the buyer approaches the sales offer.

However, there are also external influences on the customer. For example, does the current economic situation make it a good time to buy? What will other people think, colleagues at work, the family, neighbours, etc? What competing offers are around? How will my usual supplier react, etc? For some types of purchase the internal factors will outweigh the external ones. For others the reverse will be true. It is the balance between these forces which ultimately determines how the buyer will approach the buying process.

THE BUYING PROCESS

If for a moment we continue to look at the sales process from the buyer's viewpoint, it can be seen that a number of stages have to be negotiated in order to complete the process (see Figure 4.1).

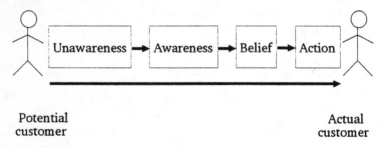

Figure 4.1   *The buying process*

Unawareness

The outset of the buying process is typified by the potential customer being blissfully unaware that the very product or service which could make his or her life easier, smarter, more productive, or whatever, is available from your company.

Awareness

The buyer becomes aware of the product or service and the company through some form of communication. This might be controlled by the supplier, for example, in the form of brochures, mail shots, advertising, PR, or salesperson visits. However, awareness might also be established by methods not controlled by the supplier, such as word of mouth recommendation, consumer articles in the press, and so on.

Clearly, those methods which offer the supplier most control over what is said to the customer cost more than the 'unofficial' voices. In contrast, a recommendation by some third party, whether a satisfied customer or an article in the paper, costs nothing … but can be worth its weight in gold.

Belief

Knowing about the product or service is one thing, believing that it will do the job which it claims is something else entirely. At this stage of the buying process the buyer's hopes, doubts and fears about the purchase have to be brought into the open, understood and satisfied with statements which can be backed up with proof, or demonstrations.

Whereas creating awareness can be a one-way communication process, creating belief is invariably a two-way process. That is to say it requires a salesperson to interact with the buyer, generally face to face, but on occasion by telephone or by letter.

Action

The process reaches its conclusion when the buyer takes action. This might be a small step, such as making a trial purchase, or it might be the placing of a significant order. Again the presence of a salesperson can help to motivate the buyer to take action and simplify any administrative matters associated with the transaction.

The general model provided by Figure 4.1 helps to provide an outline of buyer behaviour, but the more a supplying company understands about what made an impact on its previous customers, the more it can determine how to reach similar new ones more effectively. The technique for achieving this is known as customer segmentation.

CUSTOMER SEGMENTATION

It is a fact that all customers are different, yet groups of them can be shown to behave in a similar way because their motivations, needs or values are much the same. This means that if suppliers can identify such groups, they can develop an 'individual' approach which in reality is highly acceptable to everyone in that target group or segment. The benefit of doing this means that communications, pricing and general approaches to any one segment can be standardized and hence provided more cheaply. In addition, it follows that being tailored to the requirements of a specific group, what is offered and how it is communicated can become more effective.

However, there are certain rules regarding the selection of customer segments. They are:

- The customer segment must be sufficiently large to ensure that it will yield a return which justifies the expenditure incurred by developing a 'tailored approach'.
- A segment must be clearly identifiable and be capable of being described in terms which could not possibly apply to another segment.
- The basis of segmentation must have some relevance to the purchase decision or the way in which the product or service is used. For instance, it would be silly for a sandwich bar proprietor to segment customers by height, since this would have little bearing on what they bought.
- A customer segment must be reachable in order to be able to exploit and service it. Say, by chance, it might be found that a large proportion of previous customers were left-handed, retired missionaries. Unless there was a means of identifying where all the other such people who fall into this category reside, this illuminating piece of information cannot be used as a basis for segmentation.
- Ideally, the method of segmentation should be one which provides the company with some sort of competitive edge. That is to say, it plays to its unique strengths, which competitors are under pressure to match. For many companies this can take the form of a highly flexible and personalized service.

BASES FOR SEGMENTATION

There are literally hundreds of different ways of segmenting customers. Fortunately, what all these methods boil down to is a combination of three different things, segmentation on the basis of:

- What is bought
- The way customers respond or behave
- Customer characteristics

What is bought

The advantage of this approach is that it is very simple and most of the information is available in earlier sales ledgers. What happens is that a list of fairly recent customers for each product or service is compiled and then analysed to see if there are any particular common characteristics associated with customers for each product. For example, are they from particular industries or geographical locations? Are there cyclical or seasonal ordering patterns? Are customers industrial or domestic? Does order size say anything about the customers?

The idea behind this analysis is to build up a 'photo-fit' picture of a typical customer for a product or service in order to look for more of the same. The drawback with this method is that while it indicates *what* is bought, it does not really disclose *why*. Thus, it is only useful up to a point.

The way customers respond or behave

There are a number of theories which help to explain customer behaviour. Here are some of the more widely accepted approaches:

Life-style segmentation   Most people have self-images, personal aspirations and role models whom they admire. In turn, this reflects on how they dress, where they live, what they eat, where they take their holidays, and so on. The objective of this type of segmentation is to group customers (and thereby potential customers) on the basis of their outlook on life. So, for example, a financial adviser might identify one group who subscribe to long-term capital gains because this equates to security to them. However, there will be other customers who would rather see a quick, short-term advantage from their investment to fund their current life-style. The nature of the approach, advice and products with most appeal will clearly be different for each segment.

This method of segmentation works particularly well with consumer products and services.

Benefit segmentation   This operates on the thesis that customers do not buy products or services, they buy the benefits that these provide. Thus, it is not the physical characteristics of the offer (the features) which motivate buyers, but what the product or service will do for them (the benefits). On examination it will be found that not all customers seek the same benefits. It is this fact which provides the rationale for the segmentation.

For example, someone running a car showroom would find that although all the customers are looking for a vehicle, some will want one that is the safest; others will be seeking economy motoring; others will want the fastest; and others still will want the most luxurious. With such a mix of customers, the owner might ask himself if economy motoring and the luxurious end of the range could live together 'cheek by jowl'. Instead he might wish to specialize in one or the other, according to which promised to be the best business prospect. Alternatively, he might choose to split the business into two separate sites. One would provide a no-frills service for motorists with limited pockets; the other would reflect the luxurious ambience associated with the top end of the market. Needless to say, his prices would also be consistent with this strategy, with high discounts and the like at the former establishment, and prices which reflected high quality in the latter.

This example shows how the whole business can be more accurately focused if the needs of the customers are understood and those with similar requirements can be grouped together in some way.

While intellectually it is easy to grasp the idea of benefits, there is often a confusion, even among experienced salespeople, in practical terms.

Exercise 4.1	**Customer/market segmentation**

As stated earlier, segmentation is generally based upon some combination of:

- what is bought (quantities, frequency, etc)
- who buys (the type of person)
- reasons for buying (motivation).

This exercise gives you an opportunity to explore the adequacy of your current method of segmentation.

1. Write down the current method of segmentation. If you have none, consider what would be a suitable method for your particular business.
2. 'Sieve' your approach to segmentation through the following 'meshes':

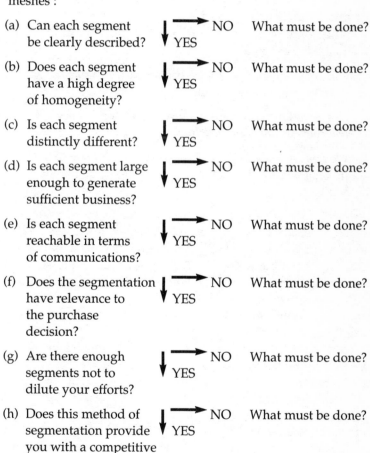

(a) Can each segment be clearly described?　　NO　What must be done?
　　　　　　　　　　　　　　YES

(b) Does each segment have a high degree of homogeneity?　　NO　What must be done?
　　　　　　　　　　　　　　YES

(c) Is each segment distinctly different?　　NO　What must be done?
　　　　　　　　　　　　　　YES

(d) Is each segment large enough to generate sufficient business?　　NO　What must be done?
　　　　　　　　　　　　　　YES

(e) Is each segment reachable in terms of communications?　　NO　What must be done?
　　　　　　　　　　　　　　YES

(f) Does the segmentation have relevance to the purchase decision?　　NO　What must be done?
　　　　　　　　　　　　　　YES

(g) Are there enough segments not to dilute your efforts?　　NO　What must be done?
　　　　　　　　　　　　　　YES

(h) Does this method of segmentation provide you with a competitive advantage?　　NO　What must be done?
　　　　　　　　　　　　　　YES

3. If your segmentation method cannot get past a particular mesh (as it should) it will be important to:

● Adapt your segmentation method so that it passes through the 'sieve'; or
● Go back to the beginning and try an entirely different approach.

Note. Only a method in which all the criteria listed above are met is likely to be successful.

4. Make a note of the segmentation approach which seems the best for your business.

Product features v benefits

The difference between features and benefits is best illustrated by the following examples:

> Our removal staff do all the packing *which means that* you don't have to worry about a thing.

> Our wooden fences are made with treated timber *which means that* they are maintenance free.

> We deliver daily *which means that* you don't have to hold stocks; in other words (which means that) you do not tie up your capital.

In each of the statements, the packing, the material treatment, the delivery schedule, are all physical characteristics of the product or service. Therefore, they are *features.* How they make impact on the customer constitutes the *benefit.* Note that the expression 'which means that' is a neat way of linking a benefit to a feature.

To check that you have indeed provided a benefit, imagine the customer asking 'so what?' in reply. Using this test on the first two examples it would seem that the benefit has been identified. After all, it would be a strange customer who wanted more worry or expensive and time-consuming fence maintenance. However, in the third example the first 'which means that' does not come up with the complete answer when given the 'so what?' test. In these circumstances the 'which means that' expression is repeated again, or paraphrased as in the example. This second attempt produces the right result when 'so what?' is asked, for what sane business person would wish to see capital tied up?

Figure 4.2 summarizes how to get from a feature to a benefit.

What happens if there is more than one benefit? Most products or services have more than one feature and so they have the potential to provide more than one benefit, as shown in Figure 4.3.

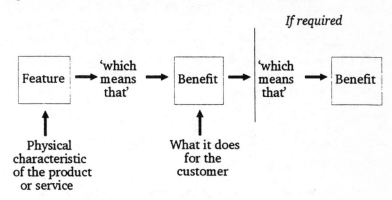

Figure 4.2   *Changing a feature to a benefit*

	Feature	Benefit	Proof
1	Call regularly	Your house appearance is always top class	Obvious
2	Fully insured	You have no risk should accidental damage occur	Show certificate
3	Long established	Can be trusted to do a good job	Quote neighbours' comments
4	Keen prices	Value for money	Quote alternative cleaners' prices

Figure 4.3   *Benefit analysis for window cleaner*

The three-column approach shown in the figure is also useful as a sales aid, since it gets the company to consider how it can prove to the customer that the promised benefit can be delivered. However, with a range of possible benefits to choose from, on which one(s) does the company capitalize? There is a simple rule to observe in these circumstances:

A 'benefit' is only a benefit if it is something the customer seeks.

It is therefore pointless to stress elements of the service or product if they are not of interest to the customer. Thus 'cheapness' is of no benefit to someone seeking 'exclusivity'; 'tried and tested' cuts no ice with someone seeking 'novelty'; and 'safety' does not appeal to the 'adventurous'. Again, the message is clear: get to know as much as you can about specific customer segments, know what they are seeking, and provide it to the best of your ability.

The exercise below will help you, in practical terms, to convert your features into benefits.

Exercise 4.2 | Features and benefits

Remember, a feature describes the product or service whereas a benefit is what the product or service does for the customer. Sometimes what is provided for the customer is concrete and measurable, for example, a reduction in processing time. It is, however, possible to provide psychological benefits such as enhanced status or pride of ownership. Neither type of benefit is intrinsically better than the other, it all depends upon what the customer seeks.

The phrase 'which means that' is a useful way of connecting a benefit to a feature. Here are two examples:

We collect our vegetables straight from the farm *which means that* they are the freshest you will find.

We are a small family business *which means that* you are not just another account, but someone who will receive our full attention and the best possible service.

Note. The first benefit stemmed from the product itself, whereas in the second example it originated from the company.

Now consider one of your main products and services and complete the following tasks:

1. Make a list of all its physical features.
2. Convert each feature into potential benefits (remember that some features might provide more than one benefit).
3. Review your list of benefits and against each one write the letter S if it is a standard benefit, something your competitors could

claim also. Alternatively, write a D if the benefit is something only you can provide, which differentiates your product or service from the rest.

4. Study what you have just written. If there are no differential benefits, consider ways that you might be able to build them in. A product or service with only standard benefits has very little to commend it.

5. If you cannot develop any differential benefits for the product, can you identify some company benefits you could exploit? The following form will help you to tackle this exercise.

NAME OF PRODUCT/SERVICE..		
FEATURES	**BENEFITS**	**TYPE OF BENEFIT**

6. Make a note of any action you will need to take as a result of the exercise.

Customer characteristics

The third and final basis for customer segmentation centres on understanding pertinent characteristics. In consumer markets these might be concerned with:

- disposable income
- social class or status
- personality types
- attitudes
- age
- gender
- regional preferences
- cultural background; and so on.

All these factors can have an influence on how customers might behave and their predilection to buy particular goods and indeed the type of outlet they would prefer to use to obtain them. In addition, this type of information can provide clues about what people read and thereby assist in finding ways of communicating with them.

For companies dealing with industrial markets, a different set of characteristics will be more useful:

● type of industry
● company size
● turnover
● main technology or production processes
● purchase pattern (such as order size and frequency)
● storage facilities
● materials handling methods etc

Figure 4.4 summarizes these three different approaches to segmentation.

What is bought	Who buys	Why
Product categories	Socio-economic factors	Life-style
Price categories	Demographics	Attitudes
Outlets	Geography	Beliefs
		Benefits
etc	etc	etc

Figure 4.4 *Bases for segmentation*

In practice, the best results are often obtained by using a combination of factors from each segmentation base, such as outlets and lifestyles, products and geographical location or demographics, and so on. It is impossible to be prescriptive regarding how segmentation should be done, but when it is tackled intelligently it can help to simplify complex situations and enable better decisions to be made regarding how to approach and win new customers.

Figure 4.5 illustrates how it might be possible to combine different forms of segment into new definitions. Starting at the top one might imagine looking through a microscope at a slide. This could be geographic, whereby one selects according to a country or county.

The next slide would depict say urban/rural or cities and towns. The third slide might be industry sectors, the fourth being size or type of ownership (public or private) and finally, perhaps, particular benefits being sought.

The line through the dots suggests that at each slide a choice has been made and finally a data base of name and addresses of potential customers is developed.

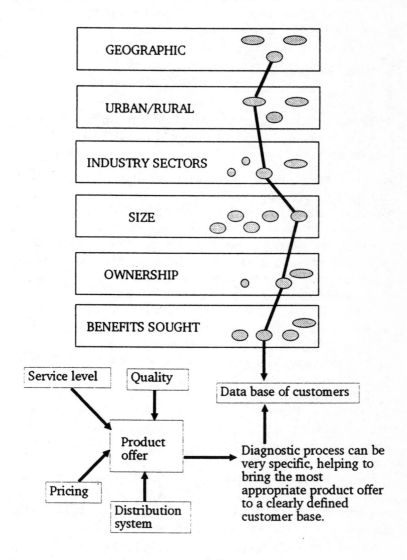

Figure 4.5 *Segmenting the market*

SIMPLE RESEARCH

Often the barrier to achieving a sensible approach to customer segmentation is due to a lack of adequate information being available to the business. As shown earlier, sales records can provide some useful information, but not all of it. Sometimes personal initiatives have to be taken by the company to obtain pieces of specialist information about customers.

This can present several problems:

- It can be expensive
- It can be time consuming
- It can often be insufficiently focused to be of use
- Unless the information is up to date it might be misleading. (*Note*. Information can deteriorate and pass its 'sell by' date just like products.)

However, being clear about what information is needed about customers or potential customers is half the battle of finding it. Clarity of purpose ensures that time is not wasted with second-rate or inferior information. There are several low-cost ways of achieving this, bearing in mind that one gram of 'hot' information (even if it is not 100 per cent accurate) is worth more than a tonne of highly accurate but out-of-date or irrelevant material. To be clear about the research, it may help to define the process.

Market research can be defined as the quantitative element. To find out how many customers, what they buy, from whom, when and so on. This will help to quantify the potential of a segment, the level of competition, trends and so on. A typical set of questions which can be used as a basis for research is provided below.

Marketing research, on the other hand, deals with the qualitative information needed to ensure that the customers' needs are understood. For example, what benefits are sought by decision makers, preference for delivery methods, payment terms, product specification, and so on.

The objective of any marketing research is to help the company to make better decisions and achieve its marketing objectives. The key to good research is to ask the right questions. While in theory this imposes no limits whatsoever, in practice the questions invariably address six distinct areas.

The market in general

Here the company might be interested in current trends, who buys what and in what quantities, the potential for existing or new products or services, and so on.

Information about products or services

For example, what do customers like about the product, what do they dislike, what improvements would they welcome, and the like.

Information about marketing methods

Here the concerns might revolve around such questions as: could we advertise differently? Do we need to review our sales methods? Do we reach our customers in the best way? Is there a better way to deliver our products or services?

Information about customers

Here the questions focus on issues such as: Who are the customers? Why do they buy? What are their interests and aspirations? Their attitudes to the product? Their image of the company?

And so on.

Information about communication media

What are the most effective ways of influencing current and potential customers?

Information about customer service

What do customers expect in terms of customer service? What do they receive? How big is the gap? Which areas should be tackled to make the most impact?

Sometimes these areas need to be investigated in order to provide ammunition to solve a specific problem. In that sense they could be considered as 'one-off' activities. However, to be successful, the company might need to monitor some of these areas on a regular, if periodic, basis.

The benefits of doing market research are:

- Subjective opinions are replaced with facts
- It can help to eliminate surprises
- Business risk is reduced
- It helps to identify how to create a competitive advantage
- It encourages the company to focus on key issues
- It identifies what marketing actions are necessary
- It can give the company confidence, knowing that it is doing the right things.

Positive though these things are, market research also costs money and will not make decisions for you. Therefore, it is wise to consider the cost/benefits of using it. For example, these questions might be asked:

- Is the information really needed?
- Is the information worth the time and effort of collecting it?
- How accurate should it be?
- How soon do we need it?
- How will it be used when we have it?

The answers to these questions will go some way to helping the company decide whether it has the expertise to collect the information itself, or if an external research agency should be used. But having said this, it is invariably on the grounds of costs that the developing organization seeks a 'do-it-yourself' approach, rather than tapping into the expertise of a specialized outsider.

However, if it is decided to use a research agency, consideration must be given to the following:

- Does it have suitably qualified staff?
- Does it have the right track record?
- Do we trust it?

Of these, the final point is probably the most significant.

There are many methods of gaining information these are just some of them.

Personal contact

The simplest way to obtain information is to ask for it. Astute business people have known this for years, and as a result have become very good listeners. What is more, they can generally get customers (or potential customers) to disclose more about themselves than they perhaps intended.

Letters or phone calls

As a rule, most people are happy to help or respond to any reasonable request, particularly if they are satisfied customers. Therefore some form of after-sales contact is not only good PR, but if used wisely can also elicit useful information about the customer's views on the product or service, and what it is like being on the receiving end of the sales process.

Questionnaires

Professional market researchers would claim with much conviction that questionnaire design is too important to be left to the 'amateur' (in principle they are correct). However, if only fairly straightforward information is required, the 'amateur' could certainly construct something with simple Yes/No answers or ticked boxes, which would yield the required information. The key issue is to be sure that those approached are genuinely representative of the group about whom the intelligence is required. Another is to ensure that the sample size is reasonably large, so that the results can be assumed to be valid.

The 'return rate' of questionnaires can be considerably increased if some incentive is provided, for example, a free gift or entry into a prize draw. The value of the information received will justify some expenditure of this nature.

Trade associations/Chambers of Commerce

Sometimes bodies such as these can be valuable sources of information regarding what is happening in specific industries or geographical regions. Reference books and business directors can be found in most public libraries which will provide addresses and phone numbers, together with outlines of their activities.

Yellow Pages, Kelly's, Kompass etc

These types of reference book can be a gold mine in terms of locating new customers. Again, they can generally be found in the larger branches of public libraries. Also, the libraries of further educational establishments carry useful reference sections to which it is usually possible to gain access on request.

Using outside researchers

This can be expensive, but again, the cost of gathering information has to be weighed against its potential for generating business. A less costly option can sometimes be arranged with a local college or business school who often seek 'projects' for their students who are attending marketing courses. Such students are generally mature and often already have a first degree, so the quality of brain power is not in question, merely if the project is compatible with their learning objectives.

Choosing between customer segments

As a result of segmenting customers and doing some simple research it is quite possible that two or three promising segments are identified. Like an army commander, the businessman would be ill-advised to dilute his resources and attempt to make in-roads in all of them. Instead, he should focus on the segment with the greatest attractiveness. What this means for one business will be different to what it means for another. One way of resolving this problem is to use the approach illustrated in Figure 4.6.

Attractiveness factors	Segment 1	Segment 2	Segment 3
Recession proof	2	3	2
Not price sensitive	5	5	2
Capacity to supply	3	6	3
Low competition	2	6	6
Quality of contacts	1	4	6
Sales potential	5	5	4
TOTAL	18	29	23

Figure 4.6 *Choosing the best customer segment*

In this example, the company listed the factors which would make a customer segment most attractive. Here the factors are that it should not be too susceptible to recession, it is not price sensitive, that its demands will be comparable with the company's resources, competition is low, there are good personal contacts, and there is a high sales potential.

Other companies might list other factors such as pay promptly, relaxed quality standards, easy to reach and so on. Attractiveness is whatever the company sees it to be.

Having established these factors, the company can score each out of 10, where 10 represents the most favourable circumstance. Using this approach it can be seen in Figure 4.6, that overall segment 2 scores best, even though it is not necessarily the most attractive on all counts, nor does it approach the maximum anywhere.

This technique can be made even more accurate if a higher points score is allocated to those factors which are perceived as being the most critical. For example, if 'not price sensitive' and 'sales potential' were the two most important factors, their scores could be doubled, or even trebled, to reflect the magnitude of that importance. The highest total score should still represent the best choice to make.

Having decided the customer segment upon which to focus, the next issue is to decide the way the products are defined, distribution channels selected, prices set and perhaps most importantly, how new customers will be approached.

Products

The product definition is likely to remain unchanged at the core, for example sticking-plaster is sticking-plaster. However, the way it is described will vary according to the benefits required. A surgeon may wish to avoid putting in stitches, a nurse may need it for ease of application, the patient for comfort, hospital management for convenient volumes and storage management and so on. To sell the same sticking-plasters through chemists, the firm will need to consider distributors' margins, attractive packaging and address any other benefits sought by retailers.

Therefore, the product may need some modification or redesigning to suit particular market segments, and so the 'surround' may change although the core is common.

Distribution

Current ways of providing the product and related services may not be suited to all customer segments. New customer segments may require the opening of depots, branches or thinking of different ways of serving the needs of potential customers.

For example, new customers in export markets will require a range of new distribution issues to be resolved, such as unit sizes, packaging, documentation and transport. Even local new customers will have requirements which may be different from existing customers, especially during the early stages of the relationship development.

Pricing

The sense of uncertainty caused by adopting a new strategy opens up opportunities as well. It may be possible, through the search for new customers, to reposition the prices to higher levels. By carefully matching the needs and expectations of the customers there will be opportunities of going in with different prices. The issues which will need to be taken into account are discussed briefly below.

Objectives   What are the objectives of the business? Is it to build market share or to find a small niche which is unattractive to competition? An aggressive approach would suggest lower prices to gain volume. (Some firms are sometimes guilty of going in with low prices without ultimately securing the larger volumes!)

New costs   In seeking new customers there are likely to be new costs, for example with repositioning the product, dealing with advertising, perhaps recruiting new staff. These costs have to be recovered through the increased volumes sold.

Time frames   Any form of change will have an impact on both the cash flow and the cost structure of a business. Therefore, the business person must decide when pay-back on new investment will be achieved and try to assess the impact of cash flow.

For example, a computer system might cost £5000. The benefits in time saved, added information, possibility of generating repeat business, etc might mean that the system recovers its own cost in about five months, while, in cash-flow terms the firm may have agreed to pay for the computer over a year. Thus it makes a positive return very quickly.

Similarly, the development of new customers will take time and the costs associated with such investment will have to be taken into account to assess whether the investment is worth while, given the pricing that might be achieved.

Service/Back-up   Prices must take account of the total cost of the transaction, including the service support and follow-up that might be necessary when exploiting new markets. The way that this information is presented and decisions about 'loss leaders' will depend on objectives and particular circumstances.

The most important element of the marketing mix, to make contact with potential new customers, is discussed next.

COMMUNICATIONS

There is a range of possibilities at the businessman's disposal. Each has strengths and weaknesses.

Advertising

Although this often has connotations of glamour, creativity and a champagne life-style in the fast lane, this is not necessarily the advertising world of the smaller company. Here, advertising can be as modest as putting cards in newsagents' windows, having an insert in a local paper, a mail-shot, or a brochure.

Sometimes breaking a rule makes more impact than conforming. Even so, the criteria related to effective advertising are shown in Figure 4.7 and companies would be well advised to follow most of

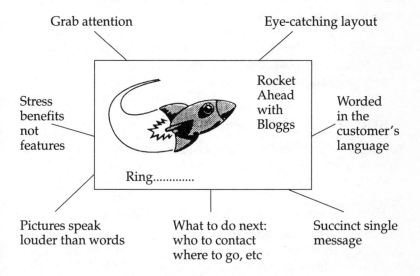

Figure 4.7 *Criteria for a good advertisement*

them if they are to make an impact. These criteria apply to virtually any message which is to be read. The critical issue is that your message is the right one.

Public relations (PR)

Many companies are getting away from the traditional approach of press releases or conferences, although that is not to decry them. The movement is more towards sponsorship in some form or other. Activities which enable the company staff to meet potential customers in relaxed surroundings are ideal. For example, sponsor the match ball at a local football club and entertain guests for the afternoon.

The nature of sponsorship ought to have some relevance to the type of business or customers with which the company deals. That is to say, with the example above, find out that they like football before proceeding.

Exhibitions

These are becoming increasingly expensive to mount, and at large trade exhibitions all the major competitors will also be in attendance, which somewhat negates any advantage the company might be wishing to establish.

There is more of a trend towards companies mounting their own exhibition in a centrally located hotel to which potential customers are invited. Some companies even have an exhibition van or lorry which travels the country.

Point-of-sale displays

Suitably positioned displays or dispensers of information can often provide an effective, low-cost means of communication.

Direct mail

This used to be a somewhat haphazard approach, but with the advent of computer technology much better results are being experienced. There are several reasons for this:

1. Target audiences can be more accurately pinpointed by renting specialist lists of people who live in particular types of neighbourhood, have particular hobbies, similar life-styles and so on. Similar information is available in an industrial context.
2. The message and the letters can be personalized.
3. The administrative costs of preparing such mail-shots are much reduced.

Personal contact

This was once a rather expensive hit or miss approach which largely relied on cold-calling. In some types of business this is still the case. However, recognizing the costs of this approach, companies have become much better at first making contact by letter or telephone, then following up the best prospects with personal calls.

It is still a fact, however, that most small businesses learn most of their information through salesperson visits, rather than advertising or the press. They are just too busy to read all the unsolicited mail sent to them.

Networking

This is based on the age-old concept, 'it isn't what you know, it's who you know'. Using this approach it is possible to reach target customers either through the agency of one's personal or business contacts or, failing this, through their contacts.

Figure 4.8 shows this process at work. Suppose the businessman has, say, ten contacts in a particular industry and they in turn each have a similar number of contacts. He now has 'personal' access to some 100 contacts. Even if only a small proportion of these are developed, they will in turn lead to even more contacts. Pursued in an intelligent way, networking can become a very powerful way of reaching customers, and it is free.

Exercise 4.3	Networking

The objective of networking is to find a path which leads to good business contacts, that is to say, people who can make decisions to buy your products or services. Often the first contacts one makes are

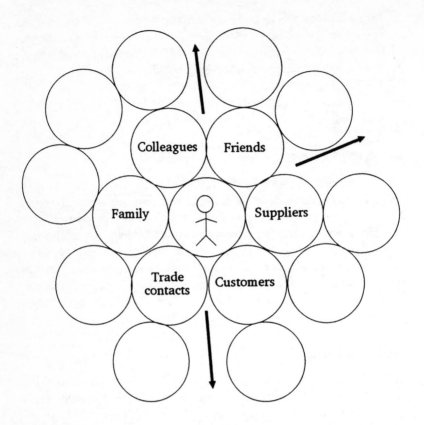

Figure 4.8 *The networking concept*

in the right place, but with the wrong people. For example, someone selling to manufacturing industry must be given a lead to the personnel manager at a company. However, a phone call to that person will quickly establish the size of the company, the exact nature of their business and, most importantly, the name of the person who needs to be seen regarding purchases.

It is worth being fairly systematic about networking and from time to time analysing the results of your efforts. This could show that some sources of contacts are better than others, or that they have led to a disproportionate amount of business being developed in a particular industry or geographical area, something you can perhaps target more formally.

Here is how a contact 'register' might look.

CONTACT SOURCES	LINKS (intermediate) contacts)	CONTACTS
Materials suppliers		
Equipment suppliers		
Family and friends		
Employees and work colleagues		
Previous satisfied customers		
Business acquaintances		
Bank and/or accountant		
Enquiries		
Chamber of Commerce		
Government services/ departments		
Delivery services		
Intermediaries, eg agents or wholesalers		
Local/trade newspapers		
Exhibitions, conferences		
Trade directories		
Rotary Club		

Make a list of contact sources by taking each contact source in turn and writing down key names, for example, Chamber of Commerce, material suppliers. Whose names spring to mind? Call them.

BUILDING A SALES PYRAMID

Experience tell us that no matter how proficient we might be at reaching customers, not every one will result in a sale. Yet if the business depends upon finding new customers for existing products or services then there must be a new 'input' of prospects each week. Extending this thinking, it is possible to construct a sales pyramid for the business, see Figure 4.9.

Here the company recognized that it needed to make a particular number of contacts per week to provide a base for the pyramid. Not every contact led to an appointment, nor indeed did every appointment lead to the salesperson being able to make a presentation, for example there might have been a misunderstanding in the previous arrangements, the contact person was not empowered to purchase, the purchase budget was exhausted, and the like. Similarly, every presentation does not lead to the company being invited to quote for the business, nor is every quotation accepted. Thus the number of actual sales (top of the pyramid) has a direct relationship to the 'input' to the 'system', the number of contacts. The conversion rate at each stage says something about the company's effectiveness.

A company which targets good prospects and is efficient in converting them to sales finishes up with a sales pyramid similar to Figure 4.10a. Its more slipshod competitor's pyramid looks more

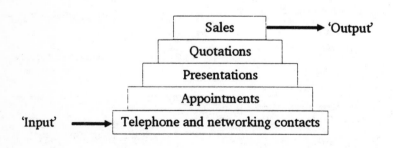

Figure 4.9 *Example of the sales pyramid*

 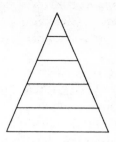

Figure 4.10a
An efficient sales organization

Figure 4.10b
An inefficient sales organization

like Fig. 4.10b. The latter has a much higher drop out at each stage of the sales process.

The value of understanding the sales pyramid is that, rather like putting petrol in a car to achieve a particular mileage, the company must continually top up its input of contacts if it is to maintain its level of sales.

All that has gone before has been provided to assist the company to identify how and where to seek the best prospects. The exercise below will help you to make the transition of turning a marketing strategy into a sales plan.

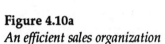

| Exercise 4.4 | Analysis of lost sales |

Although some sales might be 'lost' because you were never in a position to be able to quote for an order, these remain in the realms of the unknown. What is considered in this exercise are those situations where the customer has been met and still the business did not materialize.

1. What reasons were given by customers for not proceeding with the sale?
2. Who did win the sale?
3. What advantages did your competitors have?
4. How did competitors promote these advantages?
5. Were objections (listed in 1 above) compatible with customers' eventual choice of service/product?

6. Did you meet all members of the DMU?
7. How do you know?
8. Did you communicate effectively with all members of the DMU?
9. Did you offer the correct benefits?
10. Did you offer proof that your product/service delivers the benefits you claim?
11. Do you need to improve your selling skills?
12. Do you need better sales aids?

SUMMARY

This chapter focused almost exclusively on how a business might win new customers, for that is the essence of following this particular strategic option. For companies choosing this route there are several advantages in that the product or service life is maximized as more customers are found for it. In turn, this provides economies which are derived from experience and familiarity with producing the company output. There are also other advantages since the company is limited to no boundaries, nor is it beholden to large customers as might occur in a long-standing business relationship.

Even so, there are also some drawbacks, the major ones being that finding new customers all the time is more expensive than selling to existing ones. There is also a danger that with an undue focus on customers, the company can lose sight of the fact that its output is ageing and becoming less competitive.

In order to understand customers better it is important to look at the sales process through their eyes and see it as a buying process. The purpose of doing this is to clarify the various stages that the buyer must experience if he or she is to place an order. In other words, move from unawareness to taking action.

However, to treat every customer as a unique case can be an expensive proposition, so the idea of customer segmentation was introduced. This enables the company to group customers together so that each group is distinctly different and merits a different approach. In turn, this enables communications and the general dealings with each segment to be tailored to make optimum impact.

Although there are many approaches to segmentation, in practice they centre around three issues: What is bought? Who buys it?, and Why?

In order to answer these questions the company has recourse to its own sales records but, when these are inadequate, it must sometimes undertake some simple research. Various methods of doing this were discussed and evaluated. The end result of this type of analysis was to enable the company to select the customer segment which was most attractive, that is to say, had the best strategic fit.

The chapter finished by looking at various methods of communicating with potential customers and establishing a method of measuring the company's efficiency at converting initial contacts into actual sales.

5

Diversifying: Finding New Products and Customers

INTRODUCTION

Of all the options, diversification is in many ways the most interesting. It is the one which carries the most risks because the terra firma of known products and customers is left behind – yet, at the same time, the rewards associated with making a breakthrough in new territory can be breathtaking. This is, therefore, not a route for the faint-hearted to choose nor, as we shall show, is it the 'Last Chance Saloon' for the reckless gambler.

Like all the other business options, this particular direction has to be a matter of intelligent choice, not chance. It also depends on a high level of creativity and the skills of a juggler. Of course, there are inevitably pressures which might be tipping the scales in favour of this route. Here are just some of them.

THE PUSH FORCES

Many of the pressures will be external and originate in the circumstances surrounding the business, for example:

- Your existing customer base is shrinking rapidly
- Your products/services have reached the end of their useful life

- A key customer is lost, damaging your business irretrievably
- There is a sudden quantum shift in the market structure, for example a new major competitor enters, a new technology surfaces etc
- Someone is interested in buying you out
- Alternatively, the pressure for change might be self-generated
- You have a new business idea which ought to outscore the existing one
- You are restless and seek a new challenge
- You have inadvertently developed a new set of skills or a business 'network', which opens up entirely new horizons
- You are attracted to the idea of taking up a franchise etc.

Either singly, or in combination, some of these forces might be nigh on irresistible to fight against. Thus, the first question posed to the business owner is not about the correctness of making a choice to move in this direction, but which strategy to use (see Figure 5.1). To clarify what we mean, it will be necessary to refer back to the business directions map which was developed earlier, see Figure 1.5 (page 15).

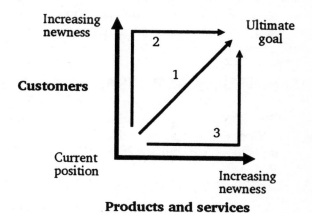

Figure 5.1 *The directions map and alternative strategies*

For a company to move from its current position to that of supplying new products or services to new customers, as Figure 5.1 shows, there are three options:

1. To move direct (route 1)

2. To reach the ultimate goal by first seeking new customers for existing products, then developing new products or services for them (route 2)

3. To develop new products/services for existing customers, then to find new markets for these (route 3).

All of these strategies are equally valid and so it is impossible to be dogmatic in recommending any one of them ahead of the other two. It will be largely a matter of personal choice for the entrepreneur and will, in all probability, be a reflection of his or her personal qualities.

The enthusiastic risk-taker will possibly favour the revolutionary, route 1 approach. In contrast, his or her more circumspect contemporaries will be likely to tend towards the evolutionary progress afforded by routes 2 and 3. Since Chapters 3 and 4 explain most of the issues involved in navigating via either of these intermediary staging posts, this chapter will focus solely on achieving this business direction by means of route 1.

Whereas the fundamental skills which underpin the two other change strategies are associated with either winning new customers, or developing new products or services, for this business strategy to succeed the key skill is to identify and exploit entirely new opportunities.

ADVANTAGES AND DISADVANTAGES

While it is difficult to be too specific about what constitutes pluses and minuses associated with this business direction (since all company situations will be different) the following seem to be distinct possibilities.

On the plus side it would seem that:

- The business can follow the most attractive opportunities
- It is not 'trapped' by its earlier history
- It can become a key player in a new field
- It can aim for business which has a much higher mark-up and/or longer-term profits than those obtainable from existing markets
- It can exploit its potential to the full.

On the down side, the business has to:

- Throw away much of its current expertise and reputation
- Develop a new customer base (which can be costly)
- Develop a new product/service (which can be risky)
- Deal with markets which are unfamiliar
- Face competition which is largely unknown
- Learn a lot in a very short time
- Have the wherewithal to invest in the new business

Taken together, it can be seen that most of the advantages are in the nature of 'jam tomorrow', whereas the disadvantages are 'here and now' costs or barriers. It is this imbalance in the portfolio of factors which makes the diversification option so risky.

Example

For most farmers in the UK, incomes from farming have been eroded and they have been forced to seek new sources of income. This has often involved moves into bed and breakfast accommodation, golf, ice cream, flowers and so on. The successful ones are those who saw themselves in a new business arena and set about analysing the market needs. The failures did not focus on customers but viewed the new businesses merely as a means of using redundant resources.

WHICH COMES FIRST, THE PRODUCT OR THE CUSTOMER?

Without a doubt many diversifications have been product led. That is to say, the product was conceived first and then new customers were found for it. This often tends to be the pattern of development of markets for high-technology based products or services. Here, each scientific breakthrough opens up new applications and hence new markets. Moreover, the time lapse between the 'invention' and its commercial application is growing ever shorter. For example, the time between the patenting of a mechanical typewriter and its general commercial application was in the order of a hundred years. In contrast to this, materials developed to overcome problems of space travel were finding commercial application within five years. Today this gap is even smaller.

Regardless of what marketing purists might say, some new markets will always open up in this way. For example, as manufacturers have become more adroit in producing microchips and integrated circuitry, they continuously seek new applications for their surplus output. What market research conducted a few years ago would have disclosed that consumers wanted teddy bears that talked? Yet today they are relatively commonplace and the technology which goes into them has become so cheap as to make these applications feasible in terms of price.

Thus, technologically aware entrepreneurs will have their eyes and ears open to learn about new developments which could be exploited. Even so, such developments will only be successful if they tap a dormant need of enough customers to sustain the business. The novelty value in itself is not sufficient, as the failure rate of new products (reckoned to be in the order of 90 per cent) bears witness.

This suggests that the safest approach to diversification is first to identify a need and then take steps to find the product or service to fill it. On balance, managing the supply side is the easiest part of the business formula; it is finding the demand which presents most organizations with their greatest problems. For this reason, we favour a customer-led approach and for most businesses this is likely to be the more successful option.

WHO ARE THE CUSTOMERS AND HOW DO YOU FIND THEM?

In fact, the astute business person does not set out to look for customers, but a need which is unfulfilled currently. This means that some market research is required initially to help identify new potential business areas. Of course, it must always be remembered that whereas the diversification is breaking new ground for the organization, it will be familiar territory for some of the other suppliers who are already active in that market. It is relatively rare, but not impossible, for a company to be the first entrant into a 'virgin' market.

The nature of the market research will, in all probability, be informal, certainly to begin with. For example, some existing customers or suppliers might complain of their difficulties in obtaining particular products or services (ones that your company would not normally supply). Alternatively, in the day-to-day running of one's own business a particular operation problem keeps recurring which could be cured using some external expertise or service if only it could be found. Then again, a chance conversation with an acquaintance might provide you with some indication that there is a new business opportunity to be tapped.

It is unsought incidents like these which often become the stimulus of a new business idea. Of course, it would be foolhardy for the organization to gamble its future on the basis of such flimsy evidence as that illustrated above. Yet, as the old adage claims, 'there is no smoke without fire'. Therefore, the next stage of research is to get to the source of the smoke-signal and to determine if it represents a feasible business opportunity.

However, what is feasible for one business person will not necessarily satisfy another. It is therefore important to be clear from the outset what it is one seeks from the new business. Is it:

- to earn more than the existing business?
- to earn enough for a comfortable living?
- to earn enough to sustain an enhanced life-style?
- to become seriously rich?

What constitutes a feasible market opportunity will certainly be different depending upon the nature of one's personal objectives. Thus, the business idea has to be translated into reasonably accurate data about market potential. Of course, market research can never entirely eliminate risk, but it can certainly help to reduce it and ensure that the best possible actions are taken.

What information is required?

Usually this will be concerned with establishing consumption trends of the product or service in the defined market. From the outset it is useful to remember that the smaller company may choose to define its market in a way that is realistic, taking into account its size and location. Thus a small corner shop might legitimately claim that its market was all potential customers who lived within a ten minute walk. In contrast, a shop which specialized in, say, photographic equipment, would be appealing to more discerning customers who would be prepared to travel some distance for the opportunity of getting expert advice and seeing all the latest gadgets associated with their hobby.

A similar rationale ought to apply to gauging market size (by area) if the company was in a different type of business where it had to deliver products or services to customers. Logistically, there will be some limits beyond which it would be difficult for the company to maintain communications or deliver, without incurring inhibitive costs. Thus, the market to be researched could be as small as a few streets, or as large as a city, region, country or even continent.

Market potential refers to the value of sales for the goods or services which could be achieved at some future date, when every person who could be a customer makes a purchase. Clearly, this state of affairs is never achieved because to do so would demand a 100 per cent conversion rate of potential to actual customers. However, the concept of market potential is still useful as a guide. It is arrived at by determining:

- the typical users of the product or service
- assessing how many like them exist in the specified market
- establishing the average price they are prepared to pay.

The market potential (in sales value terms) can be calculated by multiplying the last two factors. However in order to be successful in breaking into a new business field its size and potential are by themselves not enough.

How the market operates

Additional information which can pave the way to a successful entry into a new business arena will be in the nature of:

- Why do people buy the goods or services?
- Who makes the buying decision?
- When and where do they buy?
- Who are the most successful existing players in the market?
- Why do people choose to deal with them?
- How price sensitive is the market?

Unless you are in possession of this type of information you cannot possibly claim to understand the market, and therefore will not be able to manage the business entry successfully.

Much of this information you will be able to discover by talking to personal contacts, visiting exhibitions, posing as a potential customer to existing suppliers, and so on. Other useful information can be gathered by studying published information which is easily accessible. This might involve visiting libraries or sending off for it.

In the UK there are many sources of potentially useful information. Here are just some of them:

Aslib Directory of Information Sources in the UK
Perhaps this should be the starting point for the aspiring market researcher. Volume 1 provides an alphabetical list of all the significant sources on science, technology, and industry. This includes the names and addresses of large companies, libraries and trade associations, together with a short background and details of the information one could expect to obtain.

Annual Abstract of Statistics (Central Statistical Office, London)
This provides market size statistics in summary form, including data on demographics, the economy, construction and industrial output.

Business Monitor (Business Statistics Office, Cardiff)
This quarterly statistical report shows manufacturers' sales, imports and exports for every industry.

Trade associations
These often publish useful commercial information about specific markets. A directory of trade associations is available in most public libraries.

Dun & Bradstreet
This publication provides information regarding the size of major companies and their financial profiles.

Inter Company Comparisons, London
This is one of several organizations which sell financial performance reports of companies thereby making it possible to examine their structure, sales and profitability.

Individual company reports
These can also provide useful information about some markets.

Current British Directories
This lists all the trade directories, of which there are over 3000.

Kompass
Lists over 25,000 companies together with addresses, product codes, directors, number of employees and brief financial data.

Kelly's (Manufacturers and Merchants Volume)
Provides companies classified under product headings.

Municipal Yearbook
This provides names and addresses of all local, county and government offices in the UK.

Telephone directories and Yellow Pages
Can provide a wealth of data regarding contacts in particular industries.

This list of information sources is by no means exhaustive, but those quoted serve to illustrate that background information about many types of business can be found relatively easily on a do-it-yourself basis. In turn, they might also indicate that some further field research needs to be done, which means getting out and talking to people in order to dig deeper or using an outside research agency.

Such a combination of formal and informal research ultimately leads to the decision whether or not to diversify into a new field. If there is any doubt remaining, or difficulty in choosing between two equally attractive options, the following checklist might help in the decision making process.

1. Will the new business offer greater sales growth than the existing business?
2. Will it offer greater profit growth?
3. Is it less sensitive to price competition?
4. Is there already a lack of suppliers in the new business field?
5. Is it difficult for new competitors to set up in the business field?
6. Will the new business mean less dependency on a small number of customers than the existing business?
7. Will the new business make better use of your organizational capacity?
8. Will your business skills give you some kind of competitive edge in the new venture?

If the answer to most of these questions is 'Yes', the diversification is beginning to look like a potential winner.

SETTING UP A NEW BUSINESS?

In many ways, diversification can be equated to setting up a new business; for all intents and purposes there is little difference. This means that it will be a time-consuming activity to get the venture up and running. It will therefore need, among other things, the whole-hearted commitment of the business person since he or she is the prime mover and also the key resource.

This has a profound impact on the former business because clearly nobody can be in two places at once. Thus, while intellectually it might seem appropriate to keep the other business running until the new one is ready to take off, in practice the business person could easily fall between two stools and damage both of them. However, there are sometimes exceptions to rules and so if the old business is capable of:

- running successfully without the involvement of the owner-manager.
- not starving the new business of needed capital

then a case could be made for keeping it running while progressing with the diversification.

Sometimes what to do with the old business does not become an issue because its imminent failure is often the stimulus for seeking a new business opportunity in the first place.

What role to play?

The implied role of the businessman/owner-manager in the preceding text is that he will merely seek an opportunity to use existing management skills in a totally new business arena. In this sense his role does not change very much in the transfer from one business to the other. There are, however, other possible roles which might be more appropriate in the new business.

1. He could enter the new arena as an *investor*, that is to say with capital available to acquire an existing business in the new market. In these circumstances it then becomes a matter of

personal choice about the extent to which he becomes involved in the managerial and operational affairs of the business. It remains a possibility to operate in a 'hands-off' style and to reap the financial rewards which accrue from the investment.

2. An alternative role could be that of *inventor*, where the businessman can supply a new product or service concept to a new market. In this context he might be more interested in entering into a joint venture with an already established company who will add the 'invention' to their portfolio.

    Using this approach the businessman does not have the problems of setting up a new organization or learning about new markets but can instead profit from the creativity he brings to the venture.

Whatever role is played, the businessman is seeking a 'win-win' situation. That is one where he finishes up doing what he does (and enjoys) best, while any business associates and certainly customers also get what they seek from the new and developing relationship.

CRITICAL SUCCESS FACTORS

When it comes to taking the diversification option it is clear that the key to success is removing many of the doubts and unknowns which surround the new business. This means that the businessman has to go through a period of intense learning as preconceived notions he may have held about the new market are tested against reality. In particular this means in terms of the marketing mix.

The product or service

- There is likely to be a number of sources of ideas for new products, for example, research, scanning the media, friends, practical experience. In any of these cases, the ultimate test of viability must be clearly based on an identified need which has been researched in a particular market.

    The story of the Sony Walkman is illustrative of a creative mind that could see the opportunity of miniaturization with potential demand. Both of these insights come from long experience in the industry rather than any formal market research.

- If the product or service cannot be readily supplied by the businessman himself he should be prepared to buy in from another supplier (even one from abroad), acquire a suitable supplier, or enter some form of joint venture.
- The costing structure of any of these supplying options must be carefully calculated, since the outcome must be capable of providing consistently high margins (taking into account the prices that the new market will bear). It may be difficult to calculate the true cost of new products due to the way time may have been allocated and an element of shared services. However, clarity will be needed, especially if an injection of new funds is required from investors and banks.

Price

- Depending upon the newness of the market, the pricing structure within it might be well established or still evolving (in which case some experimentation will be required to test the price elasticity). One way to do this is to identify potential market segments clearly and to try out different prices in each.
- Although one is moving into new markets with new products, there are likely to be substitutes, complementary products or services and even competition. Therefore, the market research which is carried out will have to establish where or how to position your product against other products.
- Since sales volume is related to price, there must be an understanding of the break-even point, where a given price and a volume of sales recover the risk capital. There should also be an objective regarding the time frame in which the break-even point is reached. Without such benchmarks the success of the new venture cannot be properly monitored. These issues are dealt with in greater detail in Chapter 6.

Promotion

- A considerable amount of effort will have to go into this element of the marketing mix. Assuming one had identified a viable market segment, further detailed understanding will be required of the decision-making unit, why they buy, how they specify requirements, the dynamics of the industry they are in (for example, seasonal trends etc).

- In addition, it will be necessary to address the needs of other groups, such as influencers, opinion makers and referral sources in order to help build trust among new customers that you actually have the capacity to 'deliver' a new product.
- New channels of communication may be expensive to reach, either through networking via business clubs, former colleagues, current customers/suppliers or other contacts. Therefore, a critical element to this whole process is to allocate a budget and calculate when and how a cut-off point is reached for a decision about progressing in a given market segment.
- Since one is moving into a new setting, there may be a need to go to trade exhibitions or fairs, attend conferences, ensure press coverage and generally gain widespread exposure, to establish a corporate presence as well as sales leads, thus combining long- and short-term objectives.
- One of the key target groups with whom communication will have to be carefully managed is the government or other accredited authorities if it is needed. Approvals may be required for health and safety, technical specification, patenting, British Standards, and other criteria. The skills required to manage this group will be different from those needed to achieve sales.

Place

- Whether the product or service should be taken to the customers or vice versa will be determined by research.
- If customers need to visit to receive goods or services then location becomes an important issue, for example, easy to reach, easy to park, and so on. In addition, the premises themselves must be at least compatible with customer expectations.
- If goods or services have to be delivered then the rail/road/air infrastructure can play a significant part in the logistics of distribution.

Strategic fit

The acid test for the diversification is whether or not the owner-manager is genuinely excited and motivated by the challenge before him or her. If not, something is wrong somewhere. Whereas a manager in a large organization might be able to work to 'the book' and plan a 9.00 am to 5.00 pm existence, this approach cannot possibly work in setting up a new venture where the business person's commitment is perhaps his or her greatest asset. If entering the widget market, he or she must learn to eat, drink and sleep widgets. They can never be valued too highly, for they will pay for all the creature comforts that one day the business person hopes to possess.

The well-publicized story of Gerald Ratner the jeweller who, in an unguarded moment, proclaimed that the products he sold were 'crap', was instrumental in hastening the demise of his retail chain in an already recession-haunted consumer market. If he did not believe in and value his product, why should his customers? That is why they voted with their feet and transferred their custom elsewhere.

The risk associated with diversification is, as we have shown, the greatest of all the business direction options. If the businessman has any doubts about taking this path, perhaps that in itself is warning enough. A more evolutionary route into a new business arena must be found either through developing new products or new customers, but not both at the same time.

Diversification requires knowledge and skills in two areas – products and markets. We have covered the issues which are likely to be important in both these areas. However, the way that knowledge and skills are acquired, assuming that the businessman is not superman as well, is through one of the following ways:

- Build a team so that relevant knowledge and skills are brought in to complement those of the business. Extensive local networking in the business community or direct recruitment will be necessary.
- Seek a collaboration or joint venture with another business which has strengths in one of the areas – products or marketing. Some research, through trade associations, visits to exhibitions or other contacts will enable a short list to be developed.
- Make an acquisition of, or merger with, another business so that strengths in marketing or product knowledge can be combined with cost-reduction measures which will be positive after such a move.

All of the above strategies are attempts to reduce risks in the area of marketing a product, but carry within them other risks in the human resource and finance areas.

A key determinant in any one of the three strategies is to ensure from the very start that there is a shared vision about the future. People must know at the start why they are getting into a venture together, what they hope to gain and therefore ensure they are all pedalling in the same direction.

It is possible that each person or company is seeking a different benefit. There is nothing inherently wrong with this so long as there is not potential for a conflict of interest. In other words, it must be in everyone's interest for the venture to succeed, even if they are for slightly different reasons.

APPLICATION ACTIVITIES

Diversification as a strategy creates so many diverse needs for research. The best advice one can give is to take elements from this book and plan out a series of logical steps so that most of the ground can be covered.

You have to cover two areas of risk – customers about whom you know little and products about which you also have little knowledge.

1. Start either with potential customers or potential products and carry out a SWOT analysis (see page 10).
2. Identify ways to close the 'knowledge gap' for example, either through strategic alliances or recruiting appropriate staff.
3. Assess the risks and returns (Chapter 6).
4. Decide what market research is required.

SUMMARY

This chapter explored how the business person could pursue the strategic option of seeking both new customers and new products or services; in other words, opening up an entirely new business opportunity. Although this is clearly the most risky of the options described in this book, the circumstances surrounding some existing businesses may be such that there is no alternative but to move to a new field entirely.

If the business person decides to head out in this particular direction it is essential that he or she reduces the risk as much as possible by researching the possible new business arenas. This needs to be done for the proposed product or service in order to establish whether or not the market potential is enough to sustain a viable business. It also has to be done in order to understand the way the new market operates and to learn from the successes and failures of some of the existing players.

Market research has to be cut according to the cloth available This can mean that some of it will be conducted informally through known contacts or those recommended by friends or associates. However, it is equally possible to research much information using local reference libraries, investigating some of the potentially valuable sources of information we listed.

If the budget allows, specialist field research may need to be carried out by a suitable qualified agency.

When it comes to choosing between two possible new ventures it becomes necessary to consider a number of criteria ranging from sales and profit potential to price stability. Only after making comparisons along these lines can the final choice be made.

Another issue which was explored was the role the business person chooses to play in the new venture. Will it be as an investor, manager or inventor? The final choice will also influence the strategy for moving forward because it will indicate both the level and nature of his or her involvement in the new business.

While the diversification was likened to setting up a new business, it is possible for the business person to buy up an existing company which meets his or her requirements, or alternatively buy in the required products or services. A further possibility is to enter into a mutually beneficial joint venture with another company.

As with all the other business direction options, the critical success factors related to how the marketing mix was managed. Finally, the 'strategic fit' was considered because it is essential that the business person feels confident to go forward in this direction.

6

Financial Implications of Your Business Strategy

The previous four chapters dealt with developing action plans depending on which direction you wished to take with your business. In this chapter we will look at the financial implications of your choices. After all, there is no point in making elaborate marketing plans if, at the end of the day, the numbers do not stack up!

Often businesses avoid detailed analysis of their financial health. This may be due to an unwillingness to admit a lack of understanding of key numbers. It might also be due to the accountants' presentation of the financial position in the year-end accounts appearing to have little or no meaning for the marketing aspirations of the business.

Whatever the reason for shyness of numbers it is clearly essential that those directing the business should be more than familiar with the pulse rate affecting it, always assuming that the basic figures in the accounts are correct and up to date in the first place.

The first part of this chapter is intended for readers who are less familiar with financial analysis and terminology. Those with more experience might only need to skim through this initial text, up to the point where the strategic options are discussed (page 138).

FACTORS AFFECTING THE PULSE OF THE BUSINESS

All growing businesses have three fundamental objectives in common which allow us to see how well (or otherwise) they are doing.

1. Making a satisfactory return on investment

The first of these objectives is to make a satisfactory return (profit) on the money invested in the business. To achieve this, the return must meet four criteria:

(i) It must give a fair return to shareholders, bearing in mind the risk being taken. If the business is highly speculative and the profits are less than building society rates, you must ask if it is worth being in business.

(ii) You must make sufficient profit to allow the company to grow. If a business wants to expand it will need more working capital and eventually more space or equipment. The surest source of money for this is profits, generated by the business. A business has three sources of new money:

    (a)   the owner's money (share capital)

    (b)   loan capital, borrowed from outside sources, eg banks

    (c)   retained profits, generated by the business.

(iii) The return must be good enough to attract new investors or lenders.

(iv) The return must be at a higher level than the inflation rate to keep the real capital intact. For example, a business retaining enough profits to meet a 5 per cent growth in assets each year is in fact contracting by 5 per cent if inflation is running at 10 per cent.

2. Maintaining a sound financial base

In addition to ensuring a satisfactory return on investment, the business owner has to protect the business and him or herself from unnecessary risks, the main one being overtrading. The resulting cash-flow problem can cause a severe strain on the business, for example heavy borrowings can bring an interest burden, especially if rates rise unexpectedly.

3. Achieving growth: filling the business bucket

For the ambitious entrepreneur, growth may be the underlying objective. For others, it may be sufficient just to keep the business bucket filled. In either case they may want sales to increase, employ more people, become more efficient and improve the profits from a wider range of activities.

Whatever the short-term objective, the aim is clear, *to make a profit* which is sufficient to finance future plans.

ASSESSING THE HEALTH OF THE BUSINESS

The discipline of finance provides a plethora of analytical tools and it would be quite easy to suffer from analysis paralysis. However, there are a few key ratios (or measures) by which we can assess the health of the business. These are grouped under the following headings:

- measures of growth
- measures of profitability
- measures of liquidity.

Measures of growth

Growth can be measured in three main ways:

> sales,
> profitability; and
> number of employees.

Sales growth can be measured against a predetermined budget or against historical data. It might also be useful to measure it against competition and the level of inflation.

Often sales can be measured on the following bases:

- month by month in search of trends
- same month in this financial year compared to the last one

- percentage change on previous year or against budget/forecast
- cumulative sales
- · A rolling 12-month figure can be helpful in tracking the overall trends in the business.

Whichever method is used, the purpose of such analysis must be clear. Is it, for example, to seek out cyclical trends, overall trends or to isolate seasonal variations from an industry?

Figure 6.1 shows sales for two years of a small consulting business. It is clear that there are particular features of the business which affect sales in April and May at the lowest point and January to March at the peak, the main feature being government contracts which for budgetary reasons came to a close by the 31 March every year. It then takes time to build up again.

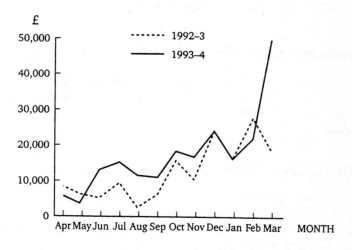

Figure 6.1   *Sales of a small consulting business (1992–4)*

Figure 6.2 shows a different picture. It is a rolling 12-month sales analysis and demonstrates a plateau at around £180,000 sales. This is due to the size of the business which has two full-time people (consultant and administrator) and two part-time people (consultant and administrator). The conclusion is that to grow the business beyond this level an additional consultant is required.

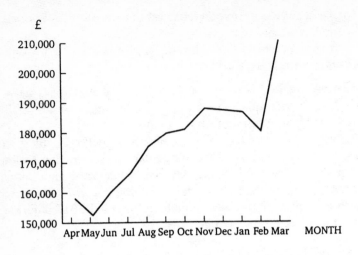

Figure 6.2 *12-month rolling sales (1993–4)*

Measures of profitability

The two main ways to measure profitability are return on capital employed and profit margins. They reveal different things about the business and therefore influence the strategies which can be pursued.

Return on capital employed (ROCE)

The financial resources employed in a business are called capital. Capital can come into a business from a number of different sources which have one thing in common: they all want a return, a percentage interest, on the money invested.

There are two particularly important ways to measure return on capital. The ROCE ratio is calculated by expressing the profit, before long-term loan interest and tax, as a proportion of the total capital employed.

$$\text{ROCE} = \frac{\text{Profit before interest and tax}}{\text{Capital employed}}$$

The main benefit of this ratio is that it provides an overall view of the business. It does not say why something might have changed in a business but does provide an overall yardstick from which to begin any analysis.

Return on shareholders' capital

The second way to assess return on capital is to calculate the profit available to shareholders.

$$\text{ROCE} = \frac{\text{Profit after tax}}{\text{Share capital and reserves}}$$

Although this ratio is not about the money actually paid out in dividends, it provides a measure of the increase in worth of the funds invested by the shareholders. If someone is considering investing in shares in the business, this ratio would be of interest.

Gearing and its effect on the business

All businesses have three main sources of money:

- their own capital (shareholders' funds)
- profits being ploughed back through reserves; and
- borrowings (debt capital).

In the latter case, businesses must pay interest irrespective of how well or badly they are performing because the lender is taking a risk and expects interest in return. If the debt capital begins to exceed the shareholders' capital and reserves, lenders usually become uncomfortable because of the difficulties in meeting interest charge commitments.

Balancing the position between equity and debt is usually very difficult for expansion but it is one of the most important aspects of finance in such a situation.

Profit margins

At a general level a measure of profit is usually calculated by subtracting all costs from sales and expressing the result as a percentage of sales.

$$\text{Gross profit margin} = \frac{\text{Sales} - \text{cost of sales}}{\text{Sales}} \times 100$$

However, for a business to benefit from management information, it is more helpful to look at profit margins in a number of more detailed ways.

This calculation provides a basic index which can be used to calculate break-even and in addition provides a measure of the health of the business. Usually, the higher the *gross margin*, sometimes called *contribution*, the higher the survivability of the business.

Table 6.1 below highlights the impact of gross profit margin on pricing decisions. For example, a firm with a present gross profit of 28 per cent giving a 5 per cent discount (minus 5 per cent) will have to generate an additional 33 per cent sales to break even. Conversely, if the firm increased prices by 5 per cent (plus 5 per cent) it can lose up to 20 per cent in sales before dropping below break-even.

A further example of a firm operating at 20 per cent gross margin and giving 10 per cent discount (minus 10 per cent) shows that sales will have to increase by 100 per cent (ie double) to break even.

The principle of gross margin calculation can be carried out with customers and products. For example, if the costs of selling to a particular customer can be calculated, it becomes possible to decide whether or not to keep that customer.

Table 6.1(a)   Effects of price reductions

	If your present margin is:								
	20%	25%	30%	35%	40%	45%	50%	55%	60%
And you reduce price by	*To produce the same exact profit, your sales volume must increase by:*								
	%	%	%	%	%	%	%	%	%
2%	11	9	7	6	5	5	4	4	3
4%	25	19	15	13	11	10	9	8	7
6%	43	32	25	21	18	15	14	12	11
8%	67	47	36	30	25	22	19	17	15
10%	100	67	50	40	33	29	25	22	20
12%	150	92	67	52	43	36	32	28	25
14%	233	127	88	67	54	45	39	34	30
16%	400	178	114	84	67	55	47	41	36
18%	900	257	150	106	82	67	56	49	43
20%	–	400	200	133	100	80	67	57	50
25%	–	–	500	250	167	125	100	83	71
30%	–	–	–	600	300	200	150	120	100

Example. Your present gross margin is 25 per cent and you cut your selling price by 10 per cent. Locate 10 per cent in the left-hand column. Now follow across to the column headed 25 per cent. You find you will need to see 67 per cent more units.

Table 6.1(b)   Effects of price reductions

	_			If you present margin is					
	20%	25%	30%	35%	40%	45%	50%	55%	60%
And you increase price by	*To produce the same exact profit, your sales volume must be reduced by:*								
	%	%	%	%	%	%	%	%	%
2%	9	7	6	5	5	4	4	4	3
4%	17	14	12	10	9	8	7	7	6
6%	23	19	17	15	13	12	11	10	9
8%	29	24	21	19	17	15	14	13	12
10%	33	29	25	22	20	18	17	15	14
12%	38	32	29	26	23	21	19	18	17
14%	41	36	32	29	26	24	22	20	19
16%	44	39	35	31	29	26	24	23	21
18%	47	42	38	34	31	29	26	25	23
20%	50	44	40	36	33	31	29	27	25
25%	56	50	45	42	38	36	33	31	29
30%	60	55	50	46	43	40	38	35	33

Source: BDO Stoy Hayward.

Sometimes businesses are tempted to chase large, prestigious clients at low margins and subsidize this strategy through more profitable but smaller clients. The example below illustrates the point.

	Single large client	%	**Six small clients**	%
	£		£	
Sales	£1,000,000	100	60,000	100
Cost of sales	85,000	85	30,000	50
Gross profit	15,000	15	30,000	50

It would appear that the smaller six clients are more profitable than the large one. A decision on whether to negotiate prices upward with the large client or add to the number of smaller clients can be taken based on this information rather than sales alone.

Similar analysis of product profitability should be carried out to ensure that the contribution being made by product justifies the effort going into it. However, care must be exercised in applying these very important tools of analysis because they only provide a single view of the business. For instance, in the example above, the six small customers may be purchasing from you only because you sell a few products at lower margins to secure profitability on others.

There is a saying, which goes as follows:

Sales is vanity
Profit is sanity; and
Cash is king

We have so far examined the first two elements of analysis. Let us now look at the third.

Measures of liquidity

The ability of a business to survive and indeed generate the cash needed to meet payments is an important element for management focus. A rather simple example makes the point. A retailer buys 10 pencils and pays £1.00 for them today. He sells them the next day, on credit, for £1.50. He then shows 50p profit in his accounts but his customer never pays up. The retailer is worse off, not just by the lost profit, but actually by the £1.00 he had to pay out.

The cycle of payments for stock, perhaps for manufacture and the payment by customers, has been likened to a merry-go-round; and the relationship between cash coming in and going out has been expressed by a series of ratios which are described next.

The short-term ability to meet commitments is calculated by the ratios between:

CURRENT ASSETS (CA)	**and**	**CURRENT LIABILITIES (CL)**
Stock		Creditors (suppliers in the main)
+ Debtors		+ Tax
+ Cash in hand at bank		+ Interest charges
TOTAL CA		TOTAL CL

$$\text{Current ratio} = \frac{\text{CA}}{\text{CL}}$$

In most industries a current ratio of 1:1 is thought to be a healthy situation because the two sides are in equilibrium. If current assets exceed current liabilities (for example, ratio 4:1) it means that the firm is in good shape and might consider how to use its assets better. On the other hand, if current liabilities are higher (for example ratio = 0.7:1) it means that the business assets may not be able to cover liabilities and some immediate attention must be given. However, this ratio is once only again part of the picture and merely opens the door to further analysis.

For those who are particularly cautious, the 'quick ratio' can be used, where only debtors and cash are taken to be 'quickly realizable' assets and are divided by current liabilities.

There are other important ratios which will have an impact on growth aspects. These are:

(a) Debtor days = $\dfrac{\text{Debtors}}{\text{Sales}} \times 365 \text{ days}$

This provides an index of the speed with which money is being collected from customers. For example, a consistent ratio of, say, 90 days would mean a slow recovery compared to a business which can collect its money in 45 days. A few methods of cash recovery are provided below.

(b) Creditor days = $\dfrac{\text{Creditors}}{\text{Purchasers}} \times 365 \text{ days}$

The result of this ratio can be compared to see if payment going out can be balanced by payment coming in from customers.

(c) Stock days = $\dfrac{\text{Stock}}{\text{Sales}} \times 365 \text{ days}$

In Japan, the holding of stock is seen as poison for the business. This is because stock is equivalent to cash on the shelves. The basic requirement is thus to speed the stock through the business quickly thereby generating sales and hence profit and cash.

Methods of improving cash flow
The following is a checklist of things to do:

Get a credit application from everyone without exception.
Give every account a credit limit.

Do not let people exceed their limit.

Make your terms of payment clear.

Do not let people go beyond your terms (not easy!).

Send accurate invoices out on time.

Send statements out at least once a month.

Have a system of reminder telephone calls and letters.

Put supplies 'on stop' to overdue customers.

Be polite to all your customers. Act promptly on queries.

Do what you say you will, for instance take legal action on Tuesday.

Know who owes you what and from when.

Know your collection performance.

Learn from people who ring *you* for money.

Keep your temper and sense of humour.

When all else fails

There are a number of recovery courses open to you when you decide you will not wait for payment to arrive in the post. These include:

- Visiting the debtor yourself. You can then assess the situation. You may decide to take your goods back if they are resaleable. Losing your profit in the sale is better than losing the debt.
- Suing the debtor yourself in the county court (or with solicitors).
- Suing the debtor in the High Court. Minimum debt £600.
- Instructing a debt collector.
- Issuing a winding-up notice or bankruptcy notice.

Cost and speed are the two main factors which will dictate the route to tread.

(Courtesy of Derek Dishman, Credit Limits, Barnet, Herts.)

Financial analysts have developed a comprehensive list of ratios and for most readers who wish to understand finance better, there are many books on the subject. The methods of analysis presented above probably represent the handful of ratios which are absolutely central to your business in general.

These ratios can be applied to make decisions regarding your strategic option. However, there is one form of analysis which is probably the most important for decision-making and that is the break-even analysis described next.

CALCULATING YOUR BREAK-EVEN POINT

A break-even chart is a very useful way to represent a company's costs and sales revenue. It shows the volume of sales required to cover the company's total costs – this is known as the break-even point.

In preparing a break-even chart, it is normal to make some simplifying assumptions. For instance, all costs are assumed to be fixed or variable.

Fixed costs are unchanged regardless of the output of the business, for example rent, rates etc. Variable costs are those that vary linearly with output, for example cost of raw materials.

Breaking even

Let us take an elementary example: a business plans to sell only one product and has only one fixed cost, the rent.

In Figure 6.3, the vertical axis shows the value of sales and costs in £000 and the horizontal shows the number of 'units' sold. The second horizontal line represent the fixed costs, those that do not change as volume increases. In this case it is the rent of £10,000. The

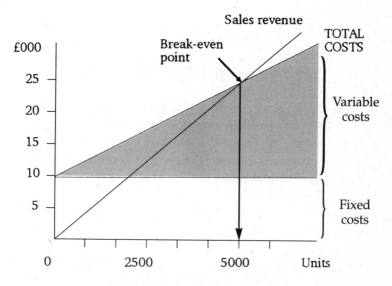

Figure 6.3   *Example break-even point*

angled line running from the top of the fixed cost line is the total cost: the fixed cost plus the variable cost of £3 per unit. Each unit we make adds £3 of variable cost, giving us the angled total cost line.

Only one element is needed to calculate the break-even point – the sales line. That is the line moving up at an angle from the bottom left-hand corner of the chart. We plan to sell at £5 per unit, so this line is calculated by multiplying the units sold by £5.

The break-even point is the stage when a business starts to make a profit. That is when the sales revenue begins to exceed both the fixed and variable costs. Figure 6.3 shows our example break-even point at 5000 units.

A formula, deduced from the chart, will save time for your own calculations.

$$\text{Break-even point} = \frac{\text{Fixed costs}}{\text{Selling price} - \text{Unit variable cost}}$$

$$\frac{£10,000}{£5 - £3} = 5000$$

It has been necessary to cover some of the basics in finance before dealing with the detail of financial implications for each of the business strategies. These are discussed next.

STRATEGY 1

STAYING MUCH THE SAME

The main issue about staying much the same is to see how much profit can be made from the same level of activity. It is assumed that, for some reason, expansion is not possible or required, yet an improvement in personal income or a need to stabilize the business calls for increased profits.

If, for example, expansion is not possible because there is insufficient capital in the business, one strategy is to take time to put the matter right, increase the savings within the business and then tackle future growth objectives.

The owner of a chain of retail chemists was considering the expansion of his business but found that this was not possible due to a lack of backing from the banks. On closer investigation he found that the net profit in his business was only 5 per cent compared to the industry average of 7 per cent. From this initial information he began to focus on analysing the costs in his business so that he could first improve the profitability, then seek to expand.

A small local coffee shop had set its prices based on competition in the area. The purchasing was done by one person (who did all the paperwork) while the selling was done in the front of the shop. No matter how hard they worked, the take-home income never seemed any better, even though they had an increasing number of customers. The reason was that the contribution margin between the cost of buying ingredients and the selling prices was just not enough.

When this factor was realized (the AH HA factor), the reaction was to negotiate harder terms with suppliers to drive down buying costs. Allied to this the selling prices were put up slightly without loss of customers.

Product/Service

Presumably, people buy from you because they can predict a level of quality or service. In order to remain the same it may be necessary to standardize your product quality (even more than, say, improving it). In this case you will need to consider the implications of changing methods and systems to achieve this. This may involve improving systems, whether these are computer-based or paper-driven, routines for dealing with orders, packaging, improving, purchasing methods. Perhaps new production methods are needed if you are a producer, or very clear systems if you are in a service business.

The aim of any reviews must be to drive down costs and to ensure consistency. The short-term financial implication will be to increase the investment in the business, for example, through upgrading computer software packages and the time lost in setting up the systems. This could be a major hurdle for some businesses, but the long-term view should be taken and the entrepreneur may well have to bite the bullet.

In any calculations for additional finance, the key is to consider whether the investment is going to add value to the balance sheet, the anticipated life of the new assets and how much difference will it make to the business.

There may be needs, such as applying for a quality standard from external sources, such as the British Standards Institute. In this case, there may be costs of additional time: yours, your employees and consultants. You should weigh up the costs of achieving the standard against the possible loss of business if you do not secure it. For instance, if the cost of achieving the standard is £20,000 and your contribution margin is 40 per cent, how much in additional sales per year will you need to recover that cost? On the other hand, how much are you likely to lose if you do not have the standard, either in the short or long term?

Promotion

If you wish to stay much the same then the communication issue is about dealing with a particular customer segment or even particular customers and ensuring that the level of communication is appropriate to the relationship.

The main cost components of this strategy will be related to maintenance of relationships. Depending on the industry in which you operate these might include:

1. Regular telephone contact
2. Regular visits
3. Regular letters or advertising in relevant media
4. Frequent appearance at conferences, press articles either on a local basis or industry specific
5. Exhibitions, local trade fairs and so on.

In each case, you have to weigh up the cost of communication and the potential increase in business needed to cover it against the possible loss of not communicating. For example, a management consultant who specializes in working for government contracts would not be taking holidays in the autumn when clients are in the process of inviting bids against tender etc. Firms dealing with manufacturing industries are used to the lull in August and may have to ensure that customers are contacted soon after their return to remind them of their relationship.

These issues will have an impact on the cash flow of the business – in terms of promotion costs and the time lag from then to the time the order comes in, and then to when the cash comes in.

Place

The distribution issue is linked firmly into concepts of the financial merry-go-round because it involves the holding of stock and its distribution. Thus speed and efficiency are critical physical activities which have direct implications on the working capital cycle (for instance, current ratio, ie CA/CI).

In staying much the same, the business has made decisions about the channels it has already established. Therefore, the key objective is to maximize returns from these channels while ensuring that they are still acceptable to customers.

One future decision must be about keeping competitors out of the channels through creating barriers to entry, for example, by the use of computer links, being the fastest, cheapest etc. The other decision needed concerns the value of the channel itself. For example, most computer manufacturers use distributors and retailers. A new entrant, Dell, decided to sell on the basis of mail order and has stormed the market place by using a new channel. The business broke the rules of distribution in the industry.

There are other factors which can determine 'place' decisions, such as location and premises. This particular aspect can have such a profound impact on the business and its marketing, and yet is probably least well understood.

In staying much the same, marginal moves may be required, exemplified by a small training business which, through lack of sound advice, signed a 20-year lease on a property. As the business expanded it came under intense pressure for increased space but was tied into an inflexible arrangement.

In other situations, businesses are tempted to buy properties which are intended as a long-term investment equivalent to a pension. While this may be a useful option for those staying much the same, it is clearly one area of financial management where good independent advice is needed.

Price

There are two objectives with pricing when staying much the same. The first is to raise margins thus making more money from the same turnover. The second is to add value to the relationship, so that the client is more 'locked-in' to you as a supplier.

Margins can be raised by increasing selling prices and by driving down cost of sales. The better the supply side is managed and the tighter the control on fixed costs, the higher the margin available to the business and its shareholders. The ratios described earlier can be used as first step to determine the margins, by looking at trends, comparing performance with previous years and with competitors.

Since customers are already doing business with you, they may be less sensitive to a modest price increase which can have such a profound impact on the ability of the business to survive and grow. The figures in Table 6.1 (pages 132–3) should be examined in more detail.

You should also consider the 'strategic fit' that you have with your customers' order of priorities. For example, a joinery business making boxes for the transport of projector lights fitted to helicopters incurs material costs of no more than £100. However, the lights cost in excess of £8000, so the packing case is an essential product for the safe transport of the light and the customer is likely to be willing to pay a high price for a well-crafted box.

In staying much the same there is a further opportunity of trying to stabilize the business with your customers, perhaps through contractual arrangements for regular supplies and payments. This may allow further opportunities for reducing costs both to yourself and your customers while, at the same time, increasing margins. Also, there will be fewer 'panics', such as missed deliveries or overdue payments etc, if business is scheduled on a regular basis.

STRATEGY 2

ADDING VALUE TO EXISTING CUSTOMERS THROUGH NEW PRODUCTS OR SERVICES

With this strategic option a certain amount of ambiguity and therefore, risk enters the equation. To start with one needs to ask why we need to introduce new products. Is it because our business is an innovator and new products are part of the business culture? For example, at 3M there is a vision to have 20 per cent of products which are new to the business every five years.

Perhaps our existing products are getting tired and, more to the point, our customers are getting tired of our existing products. Whatever the motivation for new products, the strategies employed in bringing them to the existing customers will have an impact on the finances of the business.

Product/Service

As we have asked earlier, how new is new? Are existing products to be modified or are we to add completely new products to our range? How do we describe our products, by their features or their benefits? There may be a fit between products when defined one way but not in another. For example, a range of apples from one farmer may not fit with growing cherries, unless the farmer thinks of himself as a fruit grower.

The cost implications are, therefore, based on the following choices:

- *Modification*. In some cases the cost of modification may involve simple procedures, but in others tooling-up costs may be high.
- *Buying in*. A very simple way to try to increase the volume of business with an existing client may be to buy a product or service which is new to you and offer it to existing customers. After all, they do business with you because they trust you.

   This strategy often underlies licence and joint venture deals when inventors or small businesses cannot gain access to large markets without linking up with a larger partner.

   The principle of buying in could apply equally to a product and technology and thus indeed to imports.
- *Repackage*. Existing products or services may be rebranded or packaged in some way to offer new benefits. For example, white paint could be offered as non-drip, matt, or vinyl in tins, drums and so on. Basically, it is white paint.
- *Research and development*. For some businesses, especially those which are technology based, a stream of new products is a likely strategy. It goes without saying that some sense of reality is required to ensure that these 'new products' are likely to have customers. Furthermore, the business needs to assess how 'new' they are. Do they make small improvements to existing products or are they truly new? In addition, how well do they fit the range already being offered to customers?

Many of the implications of the above list reflect additional costs, and the business having to alter the way it operates in order to sell new products to existing clients. Whichever of these options is chosen, the profitability of the decision, the cash-flow implications and the impact on the business, need to be assessed.

- *Contribution margin.* What will be the gross profit of the new product and is it in line with that of other products?
- *Modification to our systems.* What are the internal costs of handling the new product? Are there likely to be tooling costs, new brochures, training for staff, increased space requirements, alteration to computer systems, and so on.
- *Cash flow.* How will the business finance the launch of the new product? The three main sources are: the cash flowing in from existing products, borrowing either over a long term or by expanding overdraft facilities, introduction of equity, perhaps from a venture capital business or indeed, if it is in the interest of your customers some form of shared investments.

   One of the benefits of investment in new products is that sometimes it can have a positive impact on the balance sheet by adding to the net worth (eg new fixed assets), unlike promotion costs which are not seen as investments.

Promotion

If new products are to be introduced to existing customers a certain amount of additional time has to be spent in raising awareness, making the contacts within client companies and overcoming any resistance which might exist. An assessment has to be made of the following:

- What is the potential volume of sales to existing customers for the new product and, if successful, will it more than recoup the time and energy spent in prospecting?
- Over what time span will the effort have to be put in and when can we expect payback?

Based on these two questions, you can now decide the budget, in terms of time and money, that will be required to introduce new products to existing customers.

Place

The uncertainty of activities needed to be successful with new products to existing customers is reflected by decisions about distribution and location. The choices will be reflected by:

- Appropriateness of the channel to both the customer and the nature of the product.
- The need to select distributors and customers very carefully to ensure that service, back-up, etc, can be made available at the right level by your company.
- Reliability of the channel, the quality of information flows and overall effectiveness.
- Possible new methods of distribution or new locations to facilitate the supply of new products.

Most of these implications will have an impact on raising the level of fixed costs in the business. Therefore, one of the most helpful ratios to use is break-even analysis to assess what volume of sales will be needed to cover the additional costs. This would help to focus on being creative as was the case with Dell computers described earlier.

Price

Pricing decisions with new products must be based on the benefits accrued by customers. However, the business must have a clear picture of the costs. For example, new technology to help with the berthing of ships can save shipping companies and port authorities thousands of pounds. However, while oil companies may value such technology highly, owners of old ships with non-hazardous cargoes may not. Therefore, pricing will be affected by perceived value and profits.

A clear understanding of the costs, both in terms of actual product costs and the new costs of research, marketing and distribution, will help to ensure a price which can meet the business objectives.

Summarizing what has been mentioned above, some of the new costs might be:

- research and development
- tooling
- import costs

- modification costs
- finding channels of distribution
- organizing new service arrangements
- modification of other products to help fit new product into the range
- marketing research with existing clients
- advertising and promotional materials such as brochures
- staff training (or retraining).

STRATEGY 3

FINDING NEW CUSTOMERS FOR EXISTING PRODUCTS

The main objective of this strategy is to find new customers for existing products. It may be that your existing customers cannot purchase any more from you; therefore, you need to find more customers. Whatever the motivation, the key implications on costs are noted below.

Product

There are unlikely to be major cost implications to the product itself except, if we are successful in our sales effort, additional production facilities may be needed. Further, it may be necessary to modify the product slightly (for example, adding to the range of sizes or colours) or to repackage it in order to meet the needs of new market segments.

For example, computer dealers have to offer their products and services in different ways to the business community and the educational markets, where service is regarded highly enough for premium prices in one and the budget constraints force a different buying motivation on the other.

Promotion

Pursuing a strategy which seeks out new customers will clearly have cost implications. For example, a design company pitching for the work of a multinational corporation spent £69,000 on creative design time, mock-ups, presentations and follow-up. Fortunately, in this case they won the business for a two year period and recovered their investment.

Small companies sometimes have to submit to tender invitations, some of which can take up to 15 days to prepare. If time is valued at £400 per day, the cost of submitting the proposal adds up to £6000. The questions arising out of these costs of hunting are whether the resulting sales will more than cover them or not. In the second example, the business did not win the tender, merely lost 15 days which might have been better spent chasing other forms of business opportunity.

The main cost elements which affect promotion costs are:

- Customer/Market research to identify the size and potential of the market place.
- Market research, which impacts on the behaviour of buyers, identifying the benefits they seek.
- Awareness arising from attendance at exhibitions, increased advertising, press relations, direct mail, and increased travelling costs for salespeople who have to range further afield.
- Sales force recruitment and training may be an issue because to increase activity it may be necessary to employ more people.

Clearly, the recruitment of new staff poses a host of issues in addition to finance. However, we will look at these in the next chapter.

There is a saying: 'I know that 50 per cent of my advertising budget is wasted, I wish I knew which 50 per cent.' The simple solution to setting a marketing budget is to be very clear about objectives and to assess the level of revenue necessary to break even.

For example, a dried-flower business had a modest budget of £250 for a couple of advertisements each year in a glossy magazine. In order to increase sales substantially a new brochure was needed as well as increased advertising. The total needed was £8000. This is a huge jump from £250 and the business had to make an assessment of the potential sales (at a given gross margin) to see if it was worth doing. In this case it was and the business is now running at 2½ times the original size.

Usually advertising (indirect communication) has to be supplemented with a sales effort (direct or face-to-face communication).

Sales budget headings might include:

Prospecting
Market research
Buying information, data bases
Mailing, photocopying
Telephone and fax – increased costs
Staff time.

Clinching the business
Submitting proposals
Visits – car, travel expenses
Establishing accounts, new routines and procedures
Possible recruitment of new/additional staff
Training and development.

Place

The key to distribution decisions is cost/benefit analysis. Will a change in the choice of location, or method of delivering a product or service, have more or fewer benefits than the costs incurred in implementing the change?

Considerable losses are incurred in businesses through ignoring this critical cost element. For instance, a small printing firm dealing with a large demanding customer found itself frequently sending people three or four times a day to the client, to drop and collect proofs, deliver printed material, discuss new orders and so on. A little bit of foresight would have helped to reduce the ad hoc travel and improved internal efficiency.

Price

The prices set for new customers with existing products have a distinct advantage in that the cost base is probably known. The business then has to make a decision about whether it wants to try to penetrate the market with low prices, thus lowering its own costs through economies of scale, or whether to be a niche player and try to maintain high prices.

To some extent this will depend on market forces operating in each of the market segments. Pricing is going to be a fundamental management decision as it will determine the flow of cash and the profitability of the business. For small businesses the main source of finance for growth is internal, so the aim must be to obtain the highest margins consistent with market forces and product quality.

One of the benefits of investment in new products is that sometimes it can have a positive impact on the balance sheet by adding to the net worth (such as new fixed assets), unlike promotion costs which are not seen as investments.

STRATEGY 4

DIVERSIFICATION

New strategies involve the taking of risks, none more so than diversification. Risks may be classified as shown in Figure 6.4.

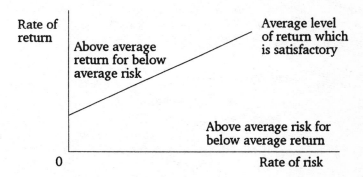

Figure 6.4   *Risks involved in diversification*

The question is, where are the risks in the proposed diversification? In the main, the forces directing choice to the right half in Figure 6.4, especially the top, may nominate the diversification.

The questions involved are broader than those represented by the 4Ps (product, place, promotion and price). The first concerns the time value of money because investment return is about speculating now to accumulate later. The table below illustrates the point.

Table 6.2 Cash flow of investment

Year	Cash out (a) £	Cash in (b) £	Net cash (b–a) £
0	50,000	–	(50,000)
1	5,000	15,000	10,000
2	5,000	15,000	10,000
3	12,500	37,500	25,000
4	12,500	37,500	25,000
5	5,000	15,000	10,000
			30,000

Table 6.2 illustrates a simple cash flow in and out over a five-year period. However, due to inflation, the profit of £30,000 may not be worth as much because the £10,000 in the fifth year or the £25,000 in the fourth may each be worth less than earlier years.

The concept which explains this erosion of value is called *present value*. It is calculated through a complex formula, which fortunately you do not need to know as tables are publicly available in books and calculators (see Table 6.3).

Table 6.3 Present value table

	Percentage			
Year	14	15	16	17
1	0.877193	0.869565	0.862069	0.854701
2	0.769468	0.756144	0.743163	0.730514
3	0.674972	0.657516	0.640658	0.624371
4	0.592080	0.571753	0.552291	0.533650
5	0.519369	0.497177	0.476113	0.456111

Table 6.4 can now be used to illustrate how much our investment is worth if we are looking for a 15 per cent return.

From this calculation we can see that the return on investment is very disappointing indeed. It presents a different view to the apparently high return when we were anticipating 60 per cent (£30,000 – £50,000) × 100

The figures we have suggest that at 15 per cent the proposition is only just worth while. By trial and error we can find out what the

Table 6.4   Net present value

Year	Net cash flow	Present value factored @ 15%	Net present value (a × b)
	(a)	(b)	
0	(50,000)	1	(50,000)
1	10,000	0.870	8,700
2	10,000	0.756	7,560
3	25,000	0.658	16,450
4	25,000	0.572	14,300
5	10,000	0.497	4,970
Net present value			£51,980

real rate of return is likely to be and then compare the result with other opportunities from which we can select. However, since we cannot see into the future we have to make a judgement based on a variety of information and not just the apparently accurate one based on two or more decimal places.

More practical considerations might include the following issues:

- How will new products or services be funded? Should the costs be assessed including or excluding a share of full costs incurred in the business?
- Market research costs will have to be considered in addition to exploring joint ventures, acquisitions of other businesses etc. This is a vast area and more specialized books will have to be consulted, in addition to taking professional advice.
- It may be necessary to recruit new staff and take expensive professional advice, all of which will have to be costed.
- Perhaps a key risk with this strategy is the dilution of management time from existing products and customers, leading to a risk of loss of business.
- Distribution and pricing decisions will depend on the nature of the diversification, the rules of the industry and the market forces.

The following group of exercises are designed to help you ask the right questions.

| Exercise 6.1 | Financial health check |

In order to gain an overview of the business you will need to carry out an overall assessment of your financial position. The checklist below brings together the lessons offered in this chapter. However, before you spend too much time with pencil and calculator, ask yourself, 'How reliable are my figures? Are they up to date? Have they been thoroughly checked by a professional accountant?'

1. Sales trends (see page 128)
2. Profitability (see page 130)
3. Gross profit margins (see page 131 and see also Table 6.1 on pages 132–3)
4. Measures of liquidity (page 134)

Assess the ratios you calculate over a period (for example, three years) to see if you can spot a trend.

You should also get hold of information about your competitors, possibly through Companies House, and run the analysis over their figures so that you can compare yourself with others. It is possible to obtain general industry information through public and business libraries (such as Dun & Bradstreet, ICC, FAME data bases) so that you can measure your business against a benchmark.

| Exercise 6.2 | Marketing related financial health checks |

The first place to look at your financial position in marketing terms is the viability of customers.

1. *Credit check your customers.* Have you assured yourself of your clients' financial viability? Are they healthy and thus can provide long-term business? How long do they take to pay? How hard do you have to work to get your cash from them?
2. *Customer profitability.* Do you achieve reasonable profit margins on the products/services you supply to your customers? Identify key clients and analyse a sample of invoices. If your gross margins are over 50 per cent to a client you should be all right, as long as your overheads are under control. Try to analyse the hidden costs of selling to a client, for example:

(a) Cost (time/resources) in preparing a proposal
(b) Following up the proposal
(c) Assuming you make the sale, how much back-up do you provide – what does it cost?

The next area of focus is product viability, primarily measured in terms of the *contribution* it makes to overheads and profits. This should be supplemented with further questions as outlined here:

1. Contribution margin of product (gross profit see page 131) now, over time, compared to other products or indeed competitors.
2. Cash flow needed to support the product in the market. Is it rising, declining?
3. Cash generated by the product. Does it exceed the amount spent on it or is it about level?
4. How does it fit in with other products in the range in terms of costs and contribution?
5. If stock is being carried, how often does it 'turn over'? How is the purchasing of materials managed – are there savings to be made.

Exercise 6.3	**Decisions about the future**

The key starting point to plan for the future is to ask if the investment will yield a higher return than just leaving the money in a bank.

Break-even analysis

The tool which can be used to make most short-term decisions is break-even analysis (page 137). For example, if you plan to increase the spend on advertising, you add this extra amount to the fixed costs, and divide by the contribution margin to see how much extra you need to sell to break even.

You can add any additional investment to the known fixed costs to see how much has to be sold to cover the high costs. For example:

- Advertising campaign
- Salesman – salary, car etc

- Extra van – purchase and running costs
- Going to an exhibition
- Moving over to use of couriers
- Extra profits or income needed by you
- Cost of market research
- Prospecting for new customers
- Introducing new products
- Patents or other forms of protecting intellectual property
- Cost of removing a product from the market
- Introducing new quality measures; and so on.

Some of the answers to the question of break-even lies in the prices at which you can sell your products and services. Exercise 6.4 will help you to identify the strengths and weaknesses related to your pricing policy.

Exercise 6.4 | Pricing

Here are a few questions which might provide you with some insights about your pricing policy.

1. What method of pricing do you use?
   (a) Cost plus
   (b) Competitive (positioned relative to competitors)
   (c) What the market will bear
   (d) Contingency (an ad hoc 'formula' based on work done)
2. Does your chosen method enable you to achieve your objectives?
3. What has been your average annual change in prices over the last three years?
4. What were the reasons for these?
5. What percentage of price increases were due to produce/ service modification designed to provide added value to the customers?
6. Does your market demand greater price flexibility than you can manage?
7. Do you use any products/services as 'loss leaders'?
8. Is there evidence that these bring in additional business?

9. What attributes of your product/service do customers value and would be willing to pay more for?
10. What attributes of your product/service do customers not value and could perhaps be eliminated in some way?

Cash flow

You should attempt a budget cash flow, showing worst, middle and best case to see what will happen to cash. This can be used to monitor the business as well as to negotiate with your bankers.

To get you started, take the basic items from a profit and loss statement and project these into the future, ensuring that you reflect cash movements only (so ignore depreciation, for example). Add to this any of your new plans to see their impact on the business. Most banks have very useful blank pro-forma sheets which can be used in case you do not have access to a spreadsheet on a computer.

RISK RETURN

Any decision which involves a new direction carries a risk. There are ways to quantify these risks so that you can make a more informed decision.

1. Cash flow of investments (page 150)
2. Calculating the present value (page 150)

In order to use the calculation of present value you will need to make a judgement about what interest rate to use. Your decision will need to take account of:

(a) Rate of inflation you forecast for the future
(b) Base interest rate
(c) The rate of return which will reflect the risk you have to take

The example here illustrates the point:

		% per year
(a)	Predicted inflation (thus the erosion of the value for money)	5
(b)	Bank lending rate over three years is, say	8
(c)	New product launch – risky but could succeed well	8
		21

So the minimum level of required return is 21 per cent and this should be used in the investment assessment of risk and return.

SUMMARY

This chapter has presented an overview of the key financial implications which arise from making specific marketing decisions. It has also highlighted some of the elements of costs incurred in pursuing a particular strategic option.

In order to integrate marketing and financial decisions we saw the need to begin with a sound understanding of the present situation of the business, in terms of financial measures of growth, profitability and liquidity.

For each strategic option, the cost implications of the four Ps has to be considered. To this end various techniques were discussed.

- When it came to new product investment or expenditure on promotion, we saw that break-even analysis can greatly assist decision-making.
- For decisions about distribution, cost/benefit analysis can be very helpful.
- In general, pricing is best geared to market conditions and, as we saw, the impact of price on margins is both powerful and immediate. Too often potential profit is thrown away by giving unnecessary discounts, even to valued customers. As the table on pages 132–3 shows, being over-generous with discounts can be catastrophic, especially when margins are low.
- When it came to diversification, a technique such as risk assessment came into its own.
- For each strategic option it is important to consider cash-flow projections that incorporate realistic revenues and costs. However, it must be remembered that money five years hence will not be worth the same as today. Thus, for time comparisons to be made, all calculations have to be converted into present-day values, using special tables.
- Finally, some financial checklists were provided to link the text with typical business situations.

7

Personnel Implications of Your Business Strategy

INTRODUCTION

It would be fruitless to write a chapter about the impact of each strategy on the personnel without first considering their effect on the owner/manager of the organization. For how he or she copes with the situation is one of the key determinants of success. Thus, how the owner manages him or herself has just as much impact as how the workforce is tackled (Figure 7.1).

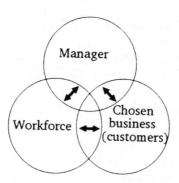

Figure 7.1   *Relationship between the business, the manager and the workforce*

As Figure 7.1 shows, the manager has a dual responsibility for both leading the workforce and making impact in the business arena. For its part, the workforce also has to make an impact in the business world, while at the same time, supplementing the initiatives and capabilities of the manager. In an ideal world, the three circles shown in Figure 7.1 would overlap to a high degree, indicating that the management and workforce are integrated and well focused on the task facing them. Sadly, this is not always the case because misunderstandings and ambiguities get in the way.

The astute manager, therefore, recognizes that success has its roots partly in how well the workforce is managed. To be a success in one area and not the other is unlikely to be a winning formula. As the company grows the pressure on the manager increases accordingly and the problem of how to make the best use of his or her time becomes a central issue. If the manager is spending too much time with customers, things might start going wrong back in the organization. Similarly, too much time spent on organizational issues means that the flow of new orders dries up or critical market information is not gathered. For some managers, this situation can be a dilemma of daunting proportions. Nevertheless, it is one which has to be resolved. The following true story suggests one possible way forward.

PLAY TO ONE'S STRENGTHS

A consultant was asked to visit a small gravel extraction company which was facing problems due to growth. On arriving at the site, he asked someone who was busy loading a lorry where he might find the manager. 'You're speaking to him,' was the reply. When loading was completed the consultant was led to a wooden hut which was the 'office'. After some preliminary discussion the manager owned up to the fact that he was so busy during the day that he could not keep up with the all the administrative paperwork. This, it emerged, he took home and worked on until the early hours of the morning. 'I'm getting very little sleep and so I'm exhausted all the time,' he complained.

The consultant then made the seemingly obvious suggestion that if another person was engaged to help load the lorries, the manager would be free to keep on top of the administration. His client appeared to agree to the logic of this, but with no great enthusiasm.

A few weeks later, when the consultant returned, his heart sank at the sight which met his eyes. There was the manager, again in his shirtsleeves, loading lorries. When he noticed his visitor, the manager stopped working and walked over to shake his hand firmly.

'Pleased to see you,' he beamed, 'that was some tremendous advice you gave me.' 'But you are still loading lorries,' said the bemused consultant. 'I know, but I love working outdoors, being with the men and seeing what's going on. I thought about what you said and recognized that I hated all the paperwork and book-keeping, so I got someone to do all of that for me. I have never been happier.'

Clearly, everyone is different in terms of the skill they possess and their personality. Some are thinkers while others prefer action. Some are capable of grasping new ideas quickly while others take longer. Some people are capable of paying great attention to detail, whereas others are inclined to want to move quickly on to something new, leaving many loose ends behind them.

Like the owner-manager in the story above, it is important to be brutally honest about one's personal strengths and, wherever possible, try to play for them. This is not as easy as it sounds because running a company often requires the manager to behave rather like the juggling act occasionally seen on television. In this, the performer starts by spinning a plate on top of a bamboo cane. Once the plate is in action he starts a second then a third, until he is rushing back and forth along a line of 12 or so, giving each cane the necessary impulse to keep its plate spinning.

However, even the most adroit juggler has limitations and needs to recognize when it is impossible to attempt to add another plate to those already in the air. Similarly, business people must learn to recognize when a task is getting out of hand. It is at this time that they must begin to specialize in what they do best and to delegate some of their other work to a well-chosen member of staff.

Exercise 7.1 | Personal planning

Each day a number of different problems surface which demand some attention. The following matrix is designed to help to prioritize the actions you should take. It is based on the assumption that issues which crop up can be either important, urgent or, perhaps, both.

High

1	2
3	4

Degree of urgency

Low

Low   **High**

Degree of importance

Box 1. Any issues which could be put into this box demand an urgent response, yet in themselves are relatively unimportant. The best way to handle these is to deal with them as they arise. If you are busy on something else at the time, delegate the new issue since it is not very important.

Box 2. Here issues are both urgent and important and, therefore, demand your full attention. They cannot be ignored.

Box 3. In contrast, the issues in this box are low priority. Fit them in when it suits you or, better still, get someone else to deal with them.

Box 4. Here the issues are important but, at present, are not urgent. There is always the temptation, because of the lack of urgency, to put them off. Unfortunately, this generally means that these issues eventually become urgent also, thereby adding to personal pressures. The best course of action with items in this box is to set some specific time aside to deal with them. So plan some time into your diary for tackling them and stick to your plan.

Unfortunately, there is evidence to suggest that the entrepreneurial personality who is so good at setting up a business is far less accommodating when it comes to delegation. It is the failure to recognize when the manager has reached his or her level of overload that can pose a serious threat to the long-term success of the business. Indeed, it is at this crisis point that many erstwhile profitable businesses begin to waver and lose their former drive and confidence.

It is because they rarely visualize a time when the enterprise becomes too complex for them to handle, that little is done regarding the development of other staff, except in the day-to-day technicalities of work. There is rarely someone who can deputize for the boss should he or she fall ill or suffer an accident. In contrast, the boss can invariably stand in for any member of staff and often has to in order to meet urgent deadlines for goods to be despatched.

Thus, the central figure can be likened to a dynamo which produces the motive power for the organization. However, the downside is the risk of a 'black-out' should he or she become overloaded or incapacitated in some way.

Exercise 7.2 is designed to help the reader to identify his or her particular skills and strengths. The questions which accompany the exercise are intended to highlight the relevance of those skills to the current business and to prompt how they might be more usefully exploited. However, this line of thinking should also lead to the consideration of whether or not the business person's lack of skills can be compensated by other staff, or if somebody should be recruited to make a better 'team' in terms of the skills portfolio.

Exercise 7.2 | Personal skills and strengths

Below is a list of personal skills and qualities. Tick all those you believe to be your strengths. Now ask yourself:

(a) Are these skills currently important for the business?
(b) In what ways could these skills be exploited?
(c) Which skills from the list represent weaknesses which need to be addressed?
(d) Which members of staff have skills which complement and add to yours?

Accounting	Creative
Administrative	Delegating
Artistic	Design
Communication	Imaginative
Co-ordinating	Interpersonal
Counselling	Inventive

Leadership	Political
Listening	Reliability
Marketing	Repairing
Mechanical	Scientific
Motivating	Selling
Negotiating	Teamwork
Organizing	Tenacity
Practical	Tolerance
Persistence	Training/Teaching
Personality	Working with numbers
Planning	Writing

The nature of the skills gap, as it might be termed, will also be related to the organizational climate. In other words, the way the company is led. The point has been made earlier that there is a considerable difference between the management approach in large companies as opposed to small ones. Table 7.1 illustrates this by considering the key result areas of any business and comparing the managerial response according to the way the company is run.

The column headed 'Professional management' is intended to convey large company attitudes and responses. Of course, some small companies are also managed in this way, particularly if the person in charge has previously worked in larger organizations.

The third column, 'Intrapreneurial management' might need some explanation. It has been found that in some large organizations, certain managers could be identified by their more swash-buckling and non-conformist approach when compared to their colleagues. They were, in fact, behaving more like entrepreneurs, but within the confines of a large business which they did not own. In many organizations such a style was found to re-energize the business and introduce much needed flexibility. It was for these reasons that 'entrepreneurs' have been actively encouraged by some organizations to the extent that it becomes 'house' style.

The two remaining columns in Table 7.1 refer to 'Entrepreneurial management' and 'Small business owner management'. Of course, the observations provided in the table are generalizations, nevertheless, it can be seen that there are slight differences between these two categories.

The former tends to be more personality dominated and is

Table 7.1 Model of management types*

Managerial type / Key Results Area	Professional management	Intrapreneurial or Entrepreneurial corporate management	Entrepreneurial management	Small business owner/ management
Profits	Explicit goal	Needed to fuel growth and to satisfy shareholders	Needed for growth	Needed for upkeep and maintenance
Planning	Formal	Long-term goals	Informal, ad hoc	Short horizons/ minimum change
Organization	Formal Explicit roles	Cross-functional teams Small units	Information with overlapping roles	Ossification of custom and practice
Control	Formal objectives Specific targets	Incentives and rewards geared to growth Control systems differ according to business area	Partial Ad hoc Rare formal measures	Inadequate No formal measurement
Management development	Planned Requirements identified and programmes designed	Strong, long-term commitment Acculturization as well as skill based programmes Multi-role work experience	Ad hoc On-the-job training	Antipathy Management development not high priority
Budgeting	Standards and variances	Varies according to business area Built-in 'slack' in budgets	Not explicit No follow-up or variance	Same as entrepreneurial management
Innovation	Incremental	Calculated risks Multiple small scale test products Winners developed to full	Calculated risks	Lacking innovativeness Risks from inaction scale

continued

Leadership	Consultative Participative	Exhortation to succeed Visionary Strong team orientation	Variable Directive to *laisser-faire* Charismatic Consultative when expedient	Directive to *laisser-faire*
Culture	Well-defined	Climate of excellence Competitive externally, collaborative internally	Dominated by personality of entrepreneur, business or industry	Family-oriented

*Shailendra Vyakarnam and Alison Rieple, 'Corporate Entrepreneurship; A Review', Cranfield School of Management Working Paper SWP 2/93

inclined to greater risk-taking than the latter. Indeed, one outstanding characteristic of the entrepreneur is the acceptance of failure as an occupational hazard rather than a reflection on his or her personal talents. Thus, the resilient entrepreneur can bounce back from disappointments and failures, still bringing a never lost enthusiasm to the new challenge ahead.

Therefore, as many management commentators are beginning to agree, 'entrepreneur' is probably the definition of a personality type, rather than a set of skills. For this reason, courses run at colleges which were designed to teach 'entrepreneurial skills' have rarely been successful. On the other hand, courses designed to encourage entrepreneurs to develop their ambitions have a much better track record. For example, one of the authors was involved in a course which encouraged participants to make better use of the information and support which was available to the small company interested in exporting. Such was the drive and commitment of those attending that, as the course progressed (there were one-day workshops each month over a four-month period), participants were selecting export markets and actually winning orders.

The following questionnaire provides an opportunity for you to assess yourself against a number of criteria related to entrepreneurship. Rather than influencing you before the event, an explanation of the questionnaire is provided at the end. All this material originates from research studies.

Exercise 7.3	Self-assessment

For the time being please go through the items mentioned and allocate a score indicating your agreement based on this scale.

Very low	Low	Medium	High	Very high
1	2	3	4	5

Please circle the number which is most appropriate to your own situation for each item. At the end you can then draw a line through these points to get an overall profile. In addition you will have the opportunity to add the scores up and measure your self assessed enterpreneurial approach.

*Developed from Kets De Vries, M F R, 'The Entrepreneurial Personality: a person at the cross-roads', *Journal of Management Studies*, Vol 14, No 1, 1977.

Section 1. How others see me

Please circle the appropriate score

I am a person others find:

1a	difficult to organize	1 2 3 4 5
1b	a powerful influence	1 2 3 4 5
1c	a person of doubtful conscience	1 2 3 4 5
1d	more anxious than average	1 2 3 4 5
1e	always keen to explore new ideas	1 2 3 4 5
1f	difficult to understand	1 2 3 4 5
1g	different and sometimes 'way out'	1 2 3 4 5
1h	somewhat impulsive	1 2 3 4 5
1i	somewhat unstable	1 2 3 4 5

Section total

Section 2. Personal perspective

I feel that I am inclined:

2a	to panic a bit when I have too much success	1 2 3 4 5
2b	to prefer a benevolent dictator style of managing	1 2 3 4 5
2c	to be uncomfortable when working for someone else	1 2 3 4 5

2d	to be anxious about making things happen	1 2 3 4 5
2e	to feel somewhat destructive at times	1 2 3 4 5
2f	to put achievement before power	1 2 3 4 5
2g	to act on my intuition and feel of the situation rather than plan carefully	1 2 3 4 5

Section total

Section 3. Beliefs

I believe that:

3a	I can materially influence the direction of a business	1 2 3 4 5
3b	I am lucky	1 2 3 4 5
3c	I can cope well with unforseseen troubles when they occur	1 2 3 4 5
3d	I am an optimist	1 2 3 4 5
3e	I am self-reliant	1 2 3 4 5
3f	I like ambiguous work problems	1 2 3 4 5
3g	I reject the conventional way of doing things	1 2 3 4 5

Section total

Section 4. Preferences

I prefer to work in a way that:

4a	enables me to take a commercial risk where I can make or lose money	1 2 3 4 5
4b	the risks go just beyond my personal experience	1 2 3 4 5
4c	I know quickly whether the risks have paid off	1 2 3 4 5
4d	I am in touch with market opportunities	1 2 3 4 5
4e	achieves results at a profit	1 2 3 4 5
4f	keeps me in control of the business	1 2 3 4 5

Section total

Section 5. Characteristics

I am the sort of person who:

5a	rarely plans ahead in a logical way	1 2 3 4 5

5b	is not too worried about getting colleagues and subordinates to agree with me before I act	1 2 3 4 5
5c	does not like to write things down too much	1 2 3 4 5
5d	is unlikely to conform with other people's view on what should be done	1 2 3 4 5
5e	usually dislikes dealing with details of a technical nature in business matters	1 2 3 4 5
5f	tends to neglect interpersonal relationships at work and offend people from time to time	1 2 3 4 5
5g	finds it difficult to be orderly, neat and tidy at work	1 2 3 4 5
5h	expects business ventures to fail from time to time, but will have another go	1 2 3 4 5
5i	enjoys the excitement, adventure and the danger of failure in taking business risks	1 2 3 4 5

Section total

Section 6. Relationships

I consider that:

6a	I have more respect for my mother than for my father	1 2 3 4 5
6b	my mother was a strong influence on my approach to business	1 2 3 4 5
6c	I am self willed	1 2 3 4 5
6d	I have few strong personal loyalties	1 2 3 4 5
6e	other people are too security conscious	1 2 3 4 5
6f	I can succeed in business where others fail	1 2 3 4 5
6g	I don't trust people too much	1 2 3 4 5
6h	I know how to influence people in business	1 2 3 4 5

Section total

Overall Score

Section 1   [   ]

Section 2   [   ]

Section 3   [   ]

Section 4	
Section 5	
Section 6	
TOTAL	

How did you score?

The above index gives you a guide based upon the available evidence of the characteristics associated with a number of entrepreneurs. Clearly, this does not describe every entrepreneur. However, it does represent a good cross-section of people who have succeeded or failed as entrepreneurs.

A high score on each of the items would be associated with the characteristics expected of many entrepreneurs. Therefore, overall if you got a score of 150 or more it is highly likely that you will have an inclination towards entrepreneurial activity. Those who scored between 120 and 150 will indeed be enterprising, but not necessarily as dedicated and committed to outright entrepreneurship as others. Those scoring between 80 and 120 will have some innovative and enterprising characteristics but are unlikely to have the outright determination to succeed as an entrepreneur. Those scoring below 80 will most likely prefer a much more secure type of job and wish to exercise influence in a different way.

Let us now take the focus off the leader for a moment and start to consider the implications of each of the strategy options for the rest of the staff.

STRATEGIC OPTION 1. STAYING MUCH THE SAME

If, as it is often claimed, people are supposed to fear change, this strategy option ought to be the easiest to manage, for essentially it is about maintaining the status quo. However, as we saw in Chapter 1, the 'steady state' is something of a myth. There are always subtle changes taking place in both the customers and the market place.

Yet, if on the surface the name of the game is stability, it actually poses quite a problem for management. For example:

- How does one keep staff motivated?

- How can complacency be kept at bay?
- What might be the basis of any reward/payment system?
- What sort of staff are best in this situation?
- What are the key skills to develop?

In some ways it is easier to deal with the last issue first because the skills required are those that underpin the organization's main task. For this strategic option it is necessary to get as close as possible to the existing customers. Thus, market intelligence is central to relationship building. The more the company knows about its customers, the better it can meet their requirements. All staff must, therefore, be made aware that future success depends upon keeping and satisfying the existing customers.

This strategy calls for an ability to build on effective relationships, requiring different skills which are embodied in three main stages:

1. *Establish rapport with the customer*
   by listening very carefully
   by empathizing
   by encouraging openness
2. *Establish credibility*
   by demonstrating an understanding of the customer's situation/business
   by selling one's expertise
   by displaying competence
3. *Build trust and confidence*
   by showing respect for the customer's interests
   by showing integrity
   by showing genuineness

All stages of this process will need to be worked at in an ongoing way. Staff who come into contact with parts of the customer organization must learn to listen hard for the customer's perceptions of the organization. This might not only be in terms of product quality but also delivery, availability, politeness and so on.

An example where this did not happen concerns a leading British supplier of fertilizer which sold mainly to farmers. Had the company listened to its customers it would have learned that the conventional plastic sacks, by which the product was delivered, were too labour intensive for farmers who operated with a minimum staff. Instead, they would prefer to have the fertilizer delivered in semi-bulk containers which could be handled by the lifting arm of a tractor. A competitor took up the farmers' suggestions and supplied the product in larger, easier to handle containers. This move damaged the original supplier to such an extent that it lost a considerable share of its market to this innovation.

The moral of this story is that the first company became complacent and believed that its customers were dependent upon it. In practice, it was the other way round.

Information about customers can be picked up by delivery people, sales office staff and any formal or informal contact. Some of the 'gossip' will be of no value, but if all information can be channelled and sifted in a routine way then some gems are bound to be discovered. It is these pieces of information which help the company to improve its service and lock itself ever closer to its customers.

Listening is not, of course, the only skill. Those who make the product or deliver the service must be encouraged to maintain quality to the highest standards. They should also be capable of identifying how and where savings can be made in the supply side of the business equation.

Since the strategic option can only offer greater profitability by adding value (and hence the prospect of raising prices) or reducing costs, cost control becomes a very important issue. From this analysis it can be seen that to underpin the operational strategy, staff who exhibit superior skills in customer service, cost control or maintaining quality, are deserving of some form of recognition either in terms of promotion or in a more materialistic form.

Motivation can be maintained and complacency reduced by continually challenging the staff to discover methods for improvement. This can be done using techniques such as 'quality circles' or informally using competitions and suggestion schemes.

STRATEGIC OPTION 2. NEW PRODUCTS FOR EXISTING CUSTOMERS

The implications for the staff regarding this option depend upon whether the new products are 'bought in' or developed by the company itself.

In the former case the staffing problems are mainly concerned with becoming familiar with the new products and setting up the appropriate administration procedures to procure and distribute these additions to the current range.

When products are developed in-house it is a quite different situation. The first skills that need to be encouraged are those of the 'detective'. Since all the products and services have to be seen as problem-solvers (they cannot possibly be successful unless they are solving a customer's problem) someone must identify new problems facing existing customers. Moreover, there must be problems which the supplying company is capable of solving and which have the potential for yielding profits.

Next the creative talents of the company must be encouraged to develop a host of possible ways to tackle this. Finally, the best solution must be chosen from among the crowd and this calls for evaluation skills.

In reality it will often be the manager/owner who is in contact with the customers and who first gets to hear about new problems. In addition, it will be he or she who decides the nature of the new product. However, power and position do not necessarily confer on a person the ability to be creative. Much to his or her chagrin, the 'boss' does not have the monopoly when it comes to good ideas. It therefore pays to identify the creative thinkers in the company. Unfortunately, it is not always an easy task because creative people are not necessarily creative all the time. Nor are there obvious clues, like the way they dress, to make identification easier.

There is a growing school of thought that avows we are all capable of being creative, it is just that many people have lost confidence in voicing their more creative ideas. Apart from the claims of some psychometric tests to predict who are the creative people, we have to fall back on more general observations. It seems that creative people have a tendency towards the following characteristics:

- They accept new ideas more readily and can be flexible in terms of work patterns and schedules
- They will probably have exhibited some form of originality in terms of managing their everyday work
- They do not tend to judge situations in black or white terms
- They readily show enthusiasm for things which interest them
- They are more likely to question organizational directives, since their attitude to authority is less compliant than average

- They are tolerant to the ideas of others and do not dismiss them out of hand.

By identifying those more inclined to be creative, it is possible to set them the task of coming up with new ideas for overcoming the emerging problems of customers. As we saw in Chapter 3, creativity is the input to innovation.

Useful though they are, creative people are, generally, less adept at converting ideas into saleable goods and services. This is the province of the practical person whose job it is to develop and plan the new addition to the company's product range.

If these skills are recognized as being important to the company pursuing this strategy, it follows that they should be rewarded in a way which is commensurate with their status. In this way the organization underpins what is important to its continued success.

STRATEGIC OPTION 3. EXISTING PRODUCTS TO NEW CUSTOMERS

In terms of the implications for personnel, this option clearly stresses the importance of first winning customers, then being capable of processing each new order swiftly and accurately. Of these it is the former which will be the critical success factor.

What makes a good salesperson?

Mention the word 'salesperson' to most people and the chances are many negative perceptions start to surface. Words like 'over-familiar', 'manipulating', 'insensitive', 'self-centred', 'pressurizing' and the like are often descriptions which can be heard. The question arises, 'Is this the truth or just popular folklore?'

By way of an answer, one of the authors recently attended a company sales conference. He knew that one of the sales representatives had an awesome record and that his commission earnings made his salary higher than the chief executive. Hoping to meet this paragon of the sales world and expecting to meet some hale and hearty, larger-than-life character in a camel-hair overcoat, the reality was a great disappointment. A small, rather shy person was sitting quietly on the sidelines seeming oblivious to all the back-slapping bonhomie of his colleagues. Was this really the record-breaker?

Indeed it was, and a few moments' conversation with him disclosed why. He didn't talk about himself, but instead encouraged the other person to talk. What is more, he listened attentively and showed a genuine interest in what was said. This was the secret of his success. He could get potential customers to talk, he listened and identified their problems and then suggested how his product would solve them. There was no trickery, misleading information or some magic technique, just a quiet conversation with somebody who *believed* he could help the customer.

It seems that the most successful sales people:

- believe in their products and services
- can quickly establish confidence and credibility
- are very good listeners
- can put themselves in the 'customer's shoes' and thereby recognize what the problems are
- sell their products on the basis of what they can do to help the customer, not what they are
- will ask for an order
- will honestly self-appraise each sales meeting in order to identify ways to improve

However, these are the face-to-face skills. Effective salespeople also know how to track down prospective clients by using simple market research such as *Yellow Pages*. They also know how to arrange appointments and thus reduce the risk of wasting time, both their own and that of an ill-chosen prospect.

Often the selling process can be reduced to a simple pyramid, Figure 7.2, the pinnacle of which is an order. Depending upon the type of business it can be shown that for every order taken, a certain number of quotations must be submitted. In turn, these depend upon so many visits to customers being made, which stem from a number of contacts being made, either by telephone or letter.

Once the sales pyramid can be established it provides a means of monitoring progress, for example if the number of new contacts falls in a particular week, the repercussions will be felt later. Similarly, the company can monitor the ratio of any two steps in the pyramid. For example:

$$\frac{\text{ORDERS}}{\text{QUOTATIONS}} \quad \text{or} \quad \frac{\text{QUOTATIONS}}{\text{VISITS}} \quad \text{or} \quad \frac{\text{VISITS}}{\text{CONTACTS}}$$

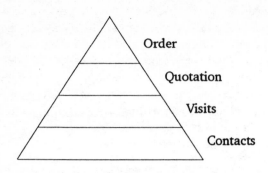

Figure 7.2   *The sales pyramid*

If, over time, it is found that any of these ratios is getting worse, then clearly it is flagging up that something is going wrong and corrective action can be taken.

Generally speaking, the most common method of rewarding salespeople is to have an element of their earnings related to performance. While in some businesses commission only is the system of payment, most companies operate with between 20 per cent and 30 per cent of income being related to meeting or exceeding sales targets.

Many companies also use indirect methods to make contact with potential customers via advertising, public relations or special promotions. For many small organizations, who are unlikely to have the necessary expertise for such activities, it can be more effective to use specialist agencies. Here the key skill is to be clear about what the objective of the communication is going to be and being capable of writing unambiguous instructions as a guide for the agency.

A third method of reaching customers is to exploit one's business contacts to get introductions. This approach is also known as networking. It works as illustrated in Figure 7.3.

The primary contacts can be existing customers, suppliers, chance contacts or even family and friends. It is likely that each can put one in touch with secondary contacts, who in turn can make introductions to further potential customers. As Figure 7.3 shows, if each contact only yielded three leads, then the initial three contacts will have led to another 27.

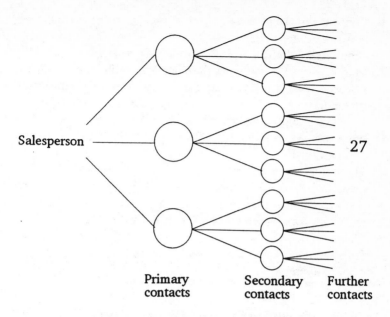

Salesperson

| Primary contacts | Secondary contacts | Further contacts |

27

Figure 7.3   *The networking concept*

The particular advantage of this process is that it is never-ending, even if some contacts fail to deliver. Another advantage is that every contact made is personalized in the sense that names can be used. For example, 'Hello, is that Mr Green? Your friend Sid Jones suggested I contact you because he believed it could be to our mutual advantage. Let me explain ...'

Networking calls for few skills except an outgoing personality and the ability to ask for contacts. Most of us conduct our private lives in this way; for example, if a clock needs repairing we will often ask friends and neighbours if they have used any local trades-people lately. Yet somehow this most natural process was ignored by businesses until relatively recently.

It is a method particularly suited to small businesses because they can develop the network at a pace which is compatible with their resources. In contrast, a successful advertising campaign might stimulate a sudden demand which the company could not possibly meet. Not only is this embarrassing, but it could also damage the company's credibility for many years to come.

There are likely to be needs for a further set of skills:

1. Computer skills to develop data bases of potential clients, with sufficient detail to be useful. There may be a need to trawl for clients and subsequently sift through for real prospects.
2. Market research skills so that one can either do some basic research oneself or have sufficient knowledge to commission the research.
3. Assistance with writing advertising and other copy so that literature going out from the organization meets customer expectations.
4. The ability to make strategic decisions regarding advertising, press relations, the development of brochures, direct mail leaflets etc, so that these supporting activities actually fit together properly with a good chance of success.
5. There is a need to balance enthusiasm for a marketing campaign with rational assessment of the potential payback, thus professional guidance may be needed.

STRATEGIC OPTION 4. NEW PRODUCTS FOR NEW CUSTOMERS

This final strategic option is the most difficult to write about in terms of its impact on personnel. In all probability, the business person would have to recruit new staff who are familiar with the new field of work. For example, a farmer who decided to use his land for a golf course would be very fortunate if his former employees were to be equally good as a teaching professional, green keeper, club secretary, bar steward and so on.

Even so, he might have one or two loyal retainers whom he might want to keep around him, for example a trusted accountant and bookkeeper or a personal secretary. In all probability the best course of action might be to recruit someone particularly experienced in the new business as a general manager, then use that person's expertise to set up the new organization.

Even considering this strategic option from the personnel perspective illustrates just how risky it is. At every twist and turn the business person is confronted with unknowns. Unless he or she is someone who thrives on ambiguity and fresh challenges, we are tempted to repeat our earlier warning to avoid this strategy and consider an alternative.

Recruiting staff

Inevitably, from time to time, new staff will have to be recruited. By being clearer about the directional strategy it should become equally clear what special skills and qualities might be required of the new person. However, the busy person running the company does not always have the luxury to reflect about objective criteria which might lead to better selection. Instead the choice will, as like as not, be made on subjective grounds, for example, 'Is this a person I could work with?', 'Is this someone I could trust?' Important though these considerations might be, as we have seen, the implications for personnel go much deeper than that.

It is for this reason that we recommend a 'framework' against which to select new staff. Such an approach will be well known to personnel specialists, but sometimes overlooked by others in the company. This approach is well tried and tested and, as will become apparent, is called 'the seven-point plan'; see Table 7.2.

By focusing on the job vacancy and thinking in turn about each factor listed in the table it becomes possible to build up an Identikit picture of the person **the job requires**. Since this process highlights what is essential for the ideal jobholder and what is merely desirable, the final analysis becomes a powerful aid to an interview. To recruit someone who does not conform to this carefully thought out specification is clearly flirting with danger.

Table 7.2   The seven-point plan

Employee specification for (job title) ....

Factor	Essential	Desirable
Physical physique: height, strength, hearing, sight, health; voice; appearance: looks, grooming, standard of dress, age, etc.		

continued

Factor	Essential	Desirable
Attainments education: level, subjects and grades; experience: nature, duration, knowledge, skills, job training, etc.		
General Intelligence test figure; creative/deductive, etc.		
Special Aptitudes mechanical; skill with words; skill with numbers; skill with hands; artistic, etc.		
Interests intellectual; practical – constructional; physical; social; artistic, etc.		
Disposition acceptability; solitary/gregarious; leader/follower; stability; attitude/authority, responsibility, etc.		
Circumstances age; dependants; wife/husband; housing; mobility/driver, etc.		

Training Plan

Unlike so many larger organizations, who often have personnel specialists staff training is rarely planned in the smaller company. To say this is not meant as a criticism, merely a statement of fact. Any training which is done is invariably learned on the job either by trial and error or by being given cursory instruction. Again, there is nothing wrong with this because often the only way we can learn about work is by doing it.

However, a recurring theme is that the main advantage the small firm has over its larger competitor is its flexibility. Yet the paradox is that because it has 'no spare fat', whenever a person is absent it is all hands to the pumps and everybody has to do their best to cover for the absentee. It is generally at this time that one of those management dicta attributable to a certain Mr Murphy begins to ring true.

One of his so-called laws states, 'If anything can go wrong it is the thing which causes most damage which goes down.' Thus, it is always the key person who is best at the key task which is required today who fails to arrive. The result? Panic.

While such periods can never be eliminated, they can sometimes be reduced by a little foresight and the use of a simple training plan, see Figure 7.4.

Key Jobs / Staff	1	2	3	4	5	6
Brown	✓		✓		✓	
Smith		✓			✓	
Bloggs		✓		✓		
Khan		✓				✓
O'Riley			✓			✓

Figure 7.4   *Example of training plan*

The first step in completing the training plan is to list the key jobs across the top of the page. The example shows only six, but there could obviously be more. In the vertical column the staff are listed. Wherever a member of staff can perform a key task to an acceptable level a (✓) is shown on the plan.

In the example provided here it becomes apparent that there is no cover for Brown regarding task 1, even though most people can take on more than one job. Similarly, task 4 is equally vulnerable because, at present, only Bloggs can do it.

In terms of planning ahead and trying to build greater flexibility into the workforce, it would pay the company, in its quieter moments, to give other people some experience on tasks 1 and 4 so that it does not have the people 'bottlenecks' that it clearly suffers from today. Used in this way a simple plan like the one illustrated can be very useful for staff development. It is easy to update and potential problem areas can be identified at a glance.

It can work equally well for a department of a larger business.

MONITORING STAFF PERFORMANCE

Selecting the best people for the jobs and then giving them the most appropriate training clearly goes a long way towards developing an effective workforce. However, from time to time it will also be important to review progress with staff who are in key positions because:

- the demands of the job might have changed
- quality standards might have drifted
- individual motivation might have reduced
- new learning needs might be surfacing.

In larger organizations these issues are usually addressed by the regular, annual, staff appraisal scheme. In smaller organizations these formal interviews are frequently neglected, sometimes by accident but often by design. Here are some of the reasons which are given to justify such lack of action:

'I know everyone here and don't need bits of paper'
'We are too small for such systems'
'We are too busy'
'It is too artificial and contrived'

'We talk about these things all the time and so don't need to set up a special event.'

Of course, there is much truth in these comments. However, since people are the key assets of the business it is worth setting some time aside in order to consider how their performance might be improved.

Confusion about role

Often one of the reasons that people underperform in a job is because they are uncertain about the scope and levels of responsibility. What follows is a procedure which is designed to eliminate such ambiguity and thereby help to focus on the key result areas of the job. One underlying assumption we have made is that the 'boss' and the 'subordinate' often have different views about the subordinate's job and what constitutes successful performance. Another is that the subordinate's performance can be enhanced or somehow lessened depending upon the actions taken by the manager. In this sense, both parties are therefore responsible for the productivity of the outcome.

1. This is conducted separately. The manager and the subordinate write a list of the tasks which make up the subordinate's job, such as staff control and maintaining quality standards.
2. Both come together and discuss their lists until agreement is reached on exactly what the job entails.
3. Separately, each rates the various tasks of the job in terms of the most important to the least important, from the point of making an impact on the company's fortunes. The most important task is rated 1, the second most important 2, and so on.
4. Both come together and discuss their ratings, until there is agreement about the relative importance of the various tasks.
5. Separately, each considers the top three tasks only, and writes down if the current level of performance is adequate or needs to be improved. Where improvement is required the two respond like this:

   The manager writes down what should be done and what actions he or she will take to help the subordinate, for example give more freedom to act, provide more resources etc.

The subordinate writes down what he or she could do if the manager in turn did certain things, such as provided more information, gave earlier warning of changes, etc.

By 'thinking' separately but 'working' together in the way illustrated above, maximum openness is brought to the situation and both parties' views are taken into consideration. With such high involvement from the subordinate, the commitment to any subsequent action plans is equally high. It is also realistic to expect the manager to invest something in the improvement plan, since it is to their mutual advantage that the plan succeeds.

Maintaining motivation

It should be fairly obvious that what constitute key areas of any job must be related to the company's overall strategy. So, for example, if new product development is the main thrust, activities like 'generating new ideas' and those which bring these ideas to life ought to be highly rated. Similarly, when the strategy is to stay much the same, activities which help to retain customers or reduce operating costs should also be recognized for their true worth.

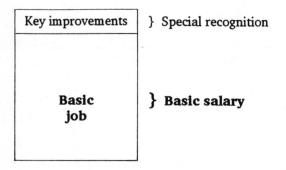

Figure 7.5 *Pay structure of job*

Thus, in terms of keeping people motivated, it makes sense to have a reward system like that illustrated in Figure 7.5. Here the individual receives a basic salary for doing the usual, day-to-day work, and some form of merit award for meeting the agreed improvement targets.

Industrial psychologists have argued loud and long regarding what constitutes the best split of 'basic' to 'merit payment'. At first sight, it would appear that the greater the element of bonus, the more incentive there would be. However, it has been found that not everyone responds to this approach. For some it is too risky having a large proportion of their income held hostage to fortune in this way. For them too much insecurity is reflected in a falling off in performance.

Others will claim that the real job satisfaction comes from the increased personal self-esteem of rising to a challenge, thus any monetary reward need only be of a token nature, a financial pat on the back at it were.

At the end of the day it seems to boil down to whether or not one thinks people are naturally lazy (and therefore need big 'bribes' to get them moving) or that they are keenly interested in the work and that is motivation enough. All that we can say is that where incentives are offered as part of a remuneration package they tend to influence about 10 to 15 per cent of the total income. The exception to this rule of thumb is with salespeople, some of whom can be employed on a commission-only basis, which means that their total income is related to performance.

Types of reward

It would be wrong to think that motivation is solely dependent upon financial rewards. There are certainly other possibilities, among which are:

- perquisites, for example company car, non-contributory pension, etc
- prizes
- vouchers
- prospect of promotion or enhanced status
- more interesting work
- training
- shares in the company
- share of the profits

Whatever the choice, psychologically speaking the reward should closely follow the time when the outstanding performance was recognized. This reinforces the concept that action leads to reward. Delay too long and this perceived link is broken.

SUMMARY

In this chapter we have considered the impact on personnel of choosing a particular directional strategy. However, the starting point was to consider the 'management style' of the business person because that made an impact on both staff and customers. The danger points were when the circumstances called for the manager to depart from his or her core strengths. It is then that competent back-up from someone else is needed. The message from this is twofold:

- managers must know their own limitations
- they must be capable of delegating to the strengths of others.

Two exercises were provided to enable the reader to explore personal strengths and weaknesses and to measure him or herself against a set of qualities which defined entrepreneurship.

The remainder of the chapter focused on issues relating to the staff as a result of choosing particular directional strategies. The chapter finished with a framework to aid better recruitment and selection and a simple plan to encourage a pro-active approach to staff training and motivation.

8

Preparing the Marketing Action Plan

INTRODUCTION

Marketing activities are subject to so many external forces that it is easy to be sidetracked and take one's eye off the ball. A marketing action plan, which outlines the reasons for action, then spells out the actions in detail taking into account the impact on finance and human resource, will help in a number of ways:

- The process of developing the plan will enable you to think about all the angles and possibilities.
- It is more likely that you will find the gaps from which you can profit.
- A written document, which you believe in, will provide a clear sense of direction for everyone involved.
- The plan will also help to act as a beacon against which you can check your direction and progress.
- The planning should involve your key staff so that there is a commitment to and understanding of the chosen direction.
- It will help to avert any wasted ad hoc advertising campaigns or misguided recruitment efforts.
- A well-thought-out plan will be a tremendous asset when approaching a bank for a loan.
- It is the process which makes dreams become reality.

The main disadvantages of preparing an action plan are that:

- The time and energy spent in its preparation could distract you from the day-to-day needs of the business.
- If you have a plan prepared by an external consultant you may find it difficult to accept because it is extremely difficult for an outsider to understand the 'culture' of the company. The result is that often a plan produced this way collects dust or is never taken seriously.
- Sometimes not enough information exists. The danger here is that people begin to treat rumours, opinions and guesses as facts, thus the resulting plan is pure fantasy ... and is potentially damaging for the business.

The preparation of a marketing action plan can be broken up into eight steps, although there may be overlaps and a need to revise decisions taken in earlier steps in the light of new information as you progress. Checklists start on page 204.

A marketing action plan is dynamic; it provides you with a structure and should include all the key tasks with dates and resource allocations demonstrating commitment to action, not just to a plan.

Figure 8.1 illustrates the logic flow in preparing the marketing action plan:

Step 1 is mostly about establishing where we are now in terms of personal/business goals, the customers and products.

Step 2 helps to identify strategic options and thus to decide which way to go.

Steps 3 to 5 are concerned with elements of choosing the best direction.

Steps 6 and 7 help to make linkages between the marketing action plan, financial implications and human resource needs.

Step 8 is the final section in which all the earlier steps are brought together by setting out a timetable, budgets and role allocation.

STEP 1. WHERE ARE YOU NOW?

What do you seek from your business?

As we discussed earlier, there are many reasons for running a business but not all that many to grow it. The influence of effective marketing can be both on sustaining your business or growing it. In either case, you need to be clear why you want to improve the marketing effort, so that you can set appropriate goals.

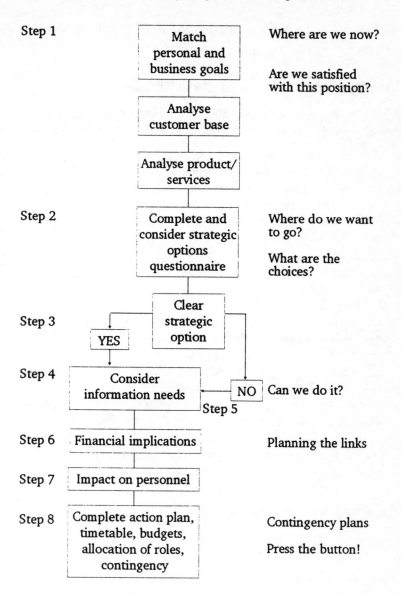

Figure 8.1 *Marketing action plan*

For example, for a business that wishes to sustain a particular position, the key objectives might be to secure business relationships at a comfortable profit margin. Another business wishing to grow might think in terms of sales volume, market share or profitability to finance expansion. Much of this is covered in Chapter 1.

Analyse your existing client base

When you know what you want from the business you can take a look at your clients. The key questions to carry out this analysis are:

- *How many active clients do you have?*
- *How much have they spent each month/year?*
- *Are they loyal?* Track your existing clients and develop a thumbnail sketch of how long they have been with you.
- *Why are they loyal to you?* It might be because your service levels are high, or at least that is what you think. On the other hand, they might be loyal because you have underpriced your products and are slow on your credit control procedures! Find out.
- *Do you make a profit on your existing customers?* Try to calculate the gross profit on a sample of invoices, large and small, to each of your major customers. Then take a cold look at the level of effort you have put in to gain and keep the client happy. If you can cost this effort and compare it with the gross profit you will soon be able to tell if the client is worth having.
- *Can you sell any more to them?* Often we forget the main asset in marketing – the existing client base. A simple question such as, 'Can we provide you with any more of our products?', or 'How much of your spend in this product area do your buy from us?' could be revealing about opportunities.

Analyse your product base

When you begin to have a clear view of customers, you then need to analyse the products.

What are the product costs? It is sometimes rather easy to assume you know the costs but a good clear audit of all the component parts of a product should provide exact figures. The example here is illustrative of a small picture-framing business.

Materials
Frame, card, glass, clips, paper, adhesives, etc.

Labour
Time for assembly and packing/presentation.

Packaging
Materials to ensure finished product is safe and well presented.

Profit Margin
To recover materials and labour
To earn a nice living
To finance growth of the business.

When you know the costs, in some detail, you can decide on how best to set your selling prices; for example, if the costs plus profit lead to a price which is well below market price, you can probably increase prices comfortably. On the other hand, if you discover that your costs exceed the price, you marketing action plan has to begin at the very basic level of business viability.

Contribution (gross profit) margin. Does your product range, on an item-by-item basis, provide a high enough profit margin? This is really fundamental to both survival and future growth. Insufficient margins are unlikely to give you or the business the freedom to choose the best strategic option because of the impact on break-even levels. Please see Chapter 6 for more detailed discussion.

Apart from viability, gross profit margins also have an impact on pricing strategies. Table 6.1 on pages 132–3 can be used to see how it is possible to affect the business by increasing or decreasing prices at different levels of profit margin. For example, a 5 per cent discount when you have only 20 per cent gross profit on a product results in the need to increase sales by 33 per cent just to break even!

Here is an illustration. Say the fixed costs are £8000 per annum. At a gross profit margin of 20 per cent the business will need to sell £8000 ÷ 20% = £40,000 to cover the fixed costs.

If a 5 per cent discount is given to secure an order against competition, the gross profit margin goes down to 15 per cent and the increase in sales needed to cover fixed costs can be calculated as follows: £8000 ÷ 15% = £53,334.00. This means the business has to find an additional £13,334.00 to compensate for the 5 per cent discount. Whether or not this is possible is another matter, but one does need to be clear about the contribution level.

Product life cycle. How fresh is your product? Is it new to the market place? New products need to fit in with other products in your range, require greater effort for introducing into the market and, indeed, will also have to fit into the overall industry. Does your product meet these criteria and are you in a position to set aside a marketing budget for it as well as a product development budget?

A product which appears to be successful because sales are growing without too much effort or where sales are substantial (if not growing), can easily lull a business into complacency. Many small businesses have fallen victim to a steady flow of income or depending on a 'cash cow' which they milk for investing in ostentatious trappings of success such as bigger cars and house plants instead of focusing on new products and customers.

A careful analysis of sales will demonstrate trends, cycles, seasons, patterns of demand from certain types of customer or into certain geographic areas. For example, a business which sold computer software into engineering firms suddenly had an order from a police department. An observant business would immediately ask how or why the product is used and why, with this new and valuable information in its possession, it could then proceed to contact other police forces from a position of strength.

Mature and declining products can cause some pain, largely because when they were successful the firm may not have invested in their replacement. Thus, there is an emotional and financial need to keep products alive which are really past their sell-by-date and should be binned – especially if they are only marginally profitable.

The 80/20 rule. In almost all walks of life this empirical rule, also known as Pareto's Law, has an impact on us – even in business. Whether as a multinational or a small business, it will be found that approximately 80 per cent of sales will come from 20 per cent of our customers.

It will be useful to carry out this analysis on your products as well as your customers, both in terms of sales and profitability. However, a word of warning here; do not rush to eliminate too many of the 80 per cent who only contribute 20 per cent of sales. Other companies have done that in the mistaken belief that they would become more efficient. Instead, they only succeeded in eliminating some of tomorrow's big customers and reduced their total sales, which had impact on unit costs.

In order to help pinpoint areas of focus and thus take the correct action, the following exercise is likely to be helpful.

Exercise 8.1	Taking the correct action

When faced with a similar situation it has been found that some people have an inclination towards taking immediate action, whereas others' initial response is to want to dig deeper and to find out what caused the events to happen. Either preference is generally put down to 'personality type'. An example of this process is shown below.

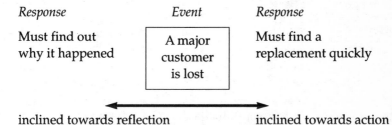

Better actions seem to come from asking 'Why?' first. For example (staying with the illustration above) by asking why, it can be discovered that the customer was lost because deliveries were unreliable. The immediate action facing the company is, therefore, to improve deliveries. Unless this is done more customers will be lost and life will be a perpetual chase to find new customers to replace dissatisfied ones.

Sometimes there is more than one reason for the problem to have surfaced. It is for this reason that asking 'Why?' can be developed into the 'Why?' diagram (Figure 8.2).

From the example in Figure 8.2 it can be seen that there are several different reasons for falling sales. The root causes which need to be addressed will lie at the end of each 'Why?' trial. (*Note*. The trails have not been taken to completion in Figure 8.2, which is intended merely to illustrate the technique. In fact, 'Why?' should keep being asked until it makes no sense to do so any further.)

Once the root causes have been discovered, action can be taken in the knowledge that it will make permanent inroads into the original problem, rather than being merely a cosmetic effect.

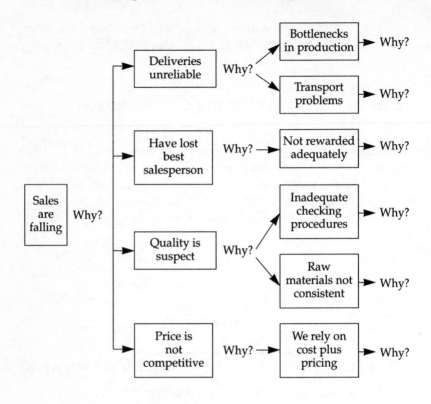

Figure 8.2   *Why? diagram*

Application activity

In order to familiarize yourself with this technique, try drawing a 'Why?' diagram for one of your company problems, then devise a simple remedial action plan.

STEP 2. ESTABLISH YOUR BUSINESS DIRECTION

When you have a clearer picture of what you want from the business you will need to audit its current marketing strengths and weaknesses. A framework like the one in Exercise 8.2 below can be very helpful and should bring together the ideas you have developed in Exercise 1.1, Selecting targets for the change effort, on page 7.

Exercise 8.2	**Strengths and Weaknesses**

This exercise enables you to take a 'snapshot' overview of your organizational strengths and weaknesses.

Measurable objectives	Major weak- ness	Needs improv- ing	Average	Useful strength	Major strength
Clear sense of direction					
Profitability					
Quality of product/ service					
Reliability of deliveries					
Technical expertise					
Flexibility					
Quality of staff					
Company image/ reputation					
Financial position					
Pricing					
Advertising					
Sales skills					
Premises					
Relationship with customers					
Relationship with suppliers					
Relationship with banks etc					
Location					
Size of operation					
Customer service					
Innovation					
Competitiveness					
Segmentation					
Market research					
Add other significant factors					

NOTE: Items you listed in the earlier force field analyses p. 8 and p. 9 can be transposed to this list.

Interpretation. In general, you will need to play to your strengths and to remedy those weaknesses which have the potential to damage the business.

You should have a look at possible directions in which to move. Exercise 1.3, Strategic options questionnaire, (page 12) will help you to assess which of four basic directions best suits your needs. These are:

1. Staying much the same
2. Taking new products to existing customers
3. Taking existing products to new customers
4. Diversification into new products and customers.

It is possible that two or more strategies might appear to be equally attractive as a result of using the questionnaire. However, you will need to focus on one – very clearly – for a given time because resources are likely to be too limited to spread thinly.

A possible set of actions might be:

- Stay where you are for 6 to 12 months, to consolidate products/customers, to ensure profitability, develop a new product or prepare the marketing action plan, recruit new staff and so on.
- Depending on the business you might then push forward either with new products or new customers. Again, if resources are limited at times, a clear focus is needed on one of these options. Operating on a too wide front results in 'busyness' but rarely a successful business. The only exception to this 'rule' could be start-up businesses which might operate with little focus because cash generation is so important, and the business has yet to establish its strengths.

   However, for a small business which is developing a marketing action plan one can argue that it is much more possible to focus on a particular strategy. A recent survey of 1350 small business ('Growth in the 1990s – Winners and Losers', Special Report 12, Paul Burns, published by 3I European Enterprise Centre, May 1994) showed that successful companies set clear objectives, whereas 'losers' constantly adapted to perceived changes in the market place.

- Circumstances will determine whether the business actually has to diversify from its current products and customers into new markets. If this is the case you may have to think of the situation as a new business with all the resultant action points, including the possible need for a business plan.

STEP 3. IF YOU HAVE A CLEAR STRATEGIC OPTION

If you have a clear grasp of the strategic option, you will also find help in preparing your action plan in one of the four chapters between 2 and 5. You should then proceed to chapters 6, 7 and 8 to help complete your marketing action plan.

STEP 4. CAN YOU DO IT?

If you are not already a user of new technology and computer systems you should consider the following options:

- Take a careful look at how information flows between you and your customers. Can communication be improved in any way by better use of faxes, phones and computers?
- Do you obtain the right information from your current systems to make effective decisions? Consider the action plans involved with each strategic option and assess your internal information system in line with what is needed.
- Consider ways in which accounting data on customers can be turned into marketing information.

Quite often the data in the accounting system is invaluable to marketing. Here are just some areas where information can be uncovered:

- understand what customers buy
- how often certain products are bought
- profit margins (per products and/or customers)
- geographic spread of clients
- payment and track record.

This data can be analysed to provide information on:

- which are the most popular products with certain clients
- which clients are increasing or decreasing their purchases from you
- how to group some clients into clusters to identify market/product segments, thus targeting future marketing effort more profitably

- how profit margin information can be used to revise prices, costs or product ranges as well as to decide on the attractiveness of certain clients
- why credit control is necessary (it is possible to keep an eye on payments far more easily).

Using the benefits of computer technology for generating management information, data can be presented visually, for example as graphs or comparative bar charts, so that trends can be identified more easily.

STEP 5. A 'WHAT IF' ANALYSIS

In case one particular strategic option is not immediately obvious because you or your firm are at a crossroads, it will be necessary for you to look at your choices in more detail and carry out a 'what if?' analysis.

To make a choice from a complex set of information may be too difficult in isolation. It might be better to seek the help of a business mentor whose judgement you trust. If such a business mentor is not readily available you should consider talking your options through with the following:

- Your accountants, although their advice on marketing may be limited. However, they should be able to help with costing and calculation of break-even, payback etc, as well as to advise you on tax implications and cash flow.
- Marketing consultants could pick up on the options and help to work through the detail of market research or sales planning. A carefully considered brief is essential to get the best out of the consultant. People who have experience of research and strategy will be best placed to understand that you need advice to help decide on a strategic direction.

    Consultants who have a narrow focus of expertise, for example in sales or advertising, may not have the full range of skills to sort out strategy. They should be able to make links to your personal goals as well as comprehend financial and human resource implications.

- Customers and suppliers with whom you have a good rapport may be able to provide useful nuggets of information so that you can decide on the right course of action.

- Business associations (Confederation of British Industry, Chamber of Commerce, other business clubs) may have useful information about opportunities which might either open new doors or tip the balance in favour of a particular strategy.
- Your general level of awareness of options and criteria for selection will increase because you are faced with a challenge. To try to resolve some of the issues you may have to go beyond the circle of contacts described above by attending exhibitions, conferences, workshops, reading journals more extensively.
- Finally, if you do not feel entirely skilled or competent in making up your mind, it may be time to attend a course or workshop to help resolve your doubts.

Some of the local business professionals, such as bank manager, colleges, libraries and government departments will know where to find a relevant course.

As part of the 'what if?' analysis it may be necessary to go back to ideas described in Step 4 to assess how information technology might help you in reaching a decision more quickly. There are some basic tips which might be helpful at this point.

1. Make a note of the options and implications.
2. Take care to have confidentiality agreements signed where relevant.
3. Put aside time and money to undertake the 'what-if?' analysis.
4. You might involve business students to help keep costs down and build links with the local community.
5. Employ outside consultants to a very clear brief otherwise you might end up paying for information you did not need.
6. Get a broad 'helicopter view' for strategic thinking, but be down-to-earth when it comes to working out the detailed implications.

STEP 6. FINANCIAL IMPLICATIONS

In business, the links between dreams and reality often come when financial implications are taken into account. Addressing financial implications of marketing strategy at this stage implies that an audit of financial resources was carried out in Step 1 or before. Therefore, the main elements of finance which have a bearing on each of the four strategic options is discussed briefly, as greater detail is provided in Chapter 6.

Each of the marketing strategy options carries with it implications for finance, which in turn will be governed by objectives and information. These are considered briefly here.

Option 1 Staying much the same

Financial objectives

- Increase profitability, strengthen cash flow.
- Reduce costs wherever possible, for example through increased efficiency.
- Increase the value of the business and/or personal pensions.

Management information

- Provide speedy, accurate information to ensure that the finger is on the pulse and indications of lowered efficiency or competitive action are picked up.

Option 2 New products to existing customers

Financial objectives

- Assess costs of new products.
- Set a budget limit for product and customer research.
- Pricing strategy to function in a niche or to gain market share.
- Establish break-even volume and payback period.
- Determine growth benefits to the business.

Management information

- Break-even analysis.
- Sensitivity analysis based on different levels of profitability and varying time-scales for success.
- Period of payback
- Cost estimates which are as accurate as possible.

Option 3 Existing products to new customers

Financial objectives

- Established detailed costs of existing products.
- Determine costs of market research and promotional campaign. Set a budget to meet anticipated/affordable costs.

- Take a view on risks/returns, bearing in mind new customers can be expensive to acquire.
- Set pricing levels according to market segments, which could be selective and high price or large volume and low price.

Management information
- Cash-flow forecast based on market research.
- Variance from budgeted costs.
- Sales and profit information on a regular basis.
- Promotional and motivational bonuses/discounts to be evaluated regularly in line with marketing and financial objectives.

Option 4 New products to new customers

To diversify fully, there must be a clear impetus since risks can be high. Thus, objectives and information will be geared to why you want to diversify and the size or level of income needed.

Financial objectives
- Determine the goals – how big a business do you want, level of profits etc.
- Determine the costs of exploring the diversification strategy and set affordable limits (budgets).

Management information
- Decision tools such as break-even, payback and internal rate of return calculations will be helpful.
- Sensitivity analysis based on 'what-if?' scenarios of a cash-flow forecast and break-even points.

STEP 7. IMPACT ON PERSONNEL

When conducting the investigation of where your business is now, it will be necessary to include an analysis of the people within. This should go beyond impressions and feelings to a clear view of skills and competencies and ambitions.

With a sound understanding it will be possible to recruit and retrain those people who are best suited to the strategic needs of the business.

Option 1 Staying much the same

This strategy calls for people who are happy to maintain the status quo and are willing to focus tightly on customer retention and thereby seek enjoyment from doing what they do well. They may not wish to have the uncertainty and ambiguity of change which results from the other three options.

In order to maximize return from staying the same, it may be necessary to introduce new technology and become more capital intensive. If this is the case the impact on personnel will be different. You will probably need to consider the following factors:

- How many employees are there?
- Is technology available to de-skill some of the tasks?
- Do we want to retain this number?
- What is the skill mix of employees?
- Is the age/gender profile of employees significant regarding actions plans?
- What reward mechanisms might best be applicable? For example, cost-reduction plans, profit maximization, corporate bonhomie etc.
- What are the skills, personalities and competencies which will be suited? For example, focus, reliability, responsiveness, contentment with status quo, eye for detail, friendly to existing customers and valuing relationships.

Option 2 New products to existing customers

The key requirements are the ability to 'listen' to customers so that new opportunities can be identified. Therefore, the need is for people who value relationships, are curious about the customer's business and interpret potential opportunities from discussions. In other words, a creative streak is needed.

To find new products one is largely reliant on internal creativity, so that new ideas flow into products. This entrepreneurial activity is about *making opportunities*. The alternative is in *taking opportunities* by finding products which already exist in other markets and adapting them in some way to meet the needs of customers.

Creative energy requires a particular type of person and, if they exist within the business, their presence will be known. If they do not, there are two options. Try to recruit someone or get help, possibly through courses, friends or business associates. Alternatively, obtain ideas and products from any number of sources: universities, other firms, journals, Patent Office, licence offers, importers/exporters etc. This is largely a scanning exercise and calls for market research skills, patience and the ability to make wide-ranging contacts. In fact, some firms advertise their desire to collaborate or find new products through specialist newsletters, journals and trade associations.

A narrow contact base is unlikely to yield much success in a scanning exercise. From quantity comes quality, therefore, in your search make allowances for travel costs and time/money spent at conferences and exhibitions.

Option 3 Finding new customers for existing products

There are, essentially, two requirements in this area; the first is to focus on getting the product or service quality right and the second is to 'hunt' for new customers.

The most frequently experienced difficulty is with internal communications between what the sales people achieve and how this is interpreted by colleagues who have to 'deliver' the service or product. Therefore, while the skills, competencies and personality are clarified for the two functions of sales and production, there is a third less clearly identified skill of co-ordination and integration.

Production or supply issues
The requirement is for people who can take pride in and deliver a high standard of product/service. They need skills related to the function as well as the ability to interpret and communicate with colleagues. Often they are unlikely to have a helicopter view of the market place since they have to respond to operational pressures.

Since their job does not call for a helicopter view they cannot or do not focus on integration issues and will need help to take a longer-term view related to the market place.

Sales issues
The skill needed in sales is the ability to take a 'No' and still bounce back to try again. In addition, the sort of person required to 'hunt' needs to have a market research skill, that is a curiosity about the client, not just a hunter mentality.

Since people in sales and marketing are in touch with customers, they can have a good global view of trends, opportunities and threats. It is essential that they are able to interpret this information into action prints for colleagues in the business. Good communication skills are essential.

Option 4 Diversification

This strategic option contains so many ambiguities that a definitive solution does not exist. However, the core element for personnel policies is to help reduce risks by finding people who can either close the gap on the customer/market front or the product/service front. For the businessman, the key competence is about building a team, temporarily or in the long term. The team can then bring specific skills and competencies into play.

STEP 8. COMPLETING THE PLAN

The final stage of putting a marketing action plan together is to deal with four specific issues: a timetable, setting a budget, allocating roles and responsibilities and having a contingency plan.

The following table provides a checklist to act as a reminder of issues and events that need to be considered to help you write up your marketing plan. If this is the first time you have attempted to put such a plan together, it is almost inevitable that there will be some teething problems. However, just like learning any other skill, the more you practise the activity, the easier it becomes. Thus, the planning process becomes easier year by year as the essential back-up information becomes more readily available.

At the end of the day, however, the success of your plan will not be due to the neatness of the figures on paper, but the quality of the thinking processes behind them.

In this book we have tried to demonstrate that it is important to think strategically over a longer time frame rather than just from minute to minute. We hope that readers will identify their organization's strengths because these are its key assets and they should be at the hub of its activities. They are also central to establishing what we have called the strategic options facing the company.

Just as a lens can focus the sun's rays with an intensity which can ignite combustible material, so can a well-devised marketing plan focus the company's capabilities to equal effect. In today's competitive climate few companies can have the luxury of trying to be all things to all customers. Instead of being journeyman builders to succeed they must become master craftsmen. This transition is not necessarily an easy one to make, but it has to be made eventually if there is going to be a future for the business.

It is something of a paradox that the more uncertain the business world, the clearer we must become about running our enterprises. The question facing most companies is therefore not, 'Should we change?', but 'How?' Only you can say, 'When?'.

If this book is successful it should also have helped you with this decision because there is really only one answer ... TODAY!

Step 1. Where are we now? (Areas to investigate)	Action (What must be done?)	Budget (Allocated as appropriate)	Start and and completion dates	Responsibility (Names of people involved)
Clarify personal/business goals				
What you seek from the business • Personal goals • Family needs (for family businesses only) • Business needs				
Analysis of your existing client base • Activity levels • Trends • Loyalty / retention • Profitability				
Analysis of product base • Detailed product costs • Materials • Labour • Service • Warranty				

- Contribution margins
- Profit objectives
- Product life cycle
- Implications of 80/20 rule

Step 2. Establish the business direction	Action	Budget	Date	Responsibilities
Selecting a strategic option - Complete and position audit (See Exercises 1.1 and 1.2) - Complete strategic options questionnaire (Exercise 1.3) - Discuss options				

Step 3. If you have a clear strategic option	Action	Budget	Date	Responsibilities
Strategic Option 1 (see Chapter 2) *Staying much the same* ● Customer research ● Building relationships with clients we need/want ● Focus on product performance ● Establish consistency of product/service ● Consider effectiveness and efficiency of distribution channels ● 80/20 rule: where is business coming from? ● Seek cost-reduction measures ● Can prices be increased to customers? ● Improve gross profit margin if possible ● Seek to strengthen the customer relations through focus on service delivery				

- Assess information needs
- Audit information needs
- Audit technology/computers, are we getting what we want?
- Financial implications
  - classify objectives
  - set out information needs
- Personnel implications
  - set out specification
  - identify future needs
  - set up recruitment procedures
  - establish retention policy
  - develop motivation and reward structure

Strategic Option 2 (see Chapter 3)
New products to existing customers
- Customer research on future increased business
  - their needs/wants
  - will they buy more from us?
- Are the customers doing well/badly?
- Identify customer segments

Action	Budget	Date	Responsibilities

Strategic Option 2 (continued)
● Are new products designed by us or do we buy in?
● Costs, performance
● Features/benefits analysis
● Assess distribution channels
● Flow of information needed
● Pricing objectives
● Competitive activity
● Develop communication plan
  – awareness building
 	
Strategic Option 3 (see Chapter 4)
Existing products to new customers
  – creating interest and sales
  – possible option-advertising, sales visits, direct mail, exhibitions etc
● Calculate profit margins, set clear goals
● Assess break-even levels			

- Programme cash-flow forecast
- Negotiate additional finance if required
- Establish good information system
- Brief colleagues on objectives
- Focus on communication skills of staff
- Reward creativity – value added behaviour
- Other ...
- Initiate market research activity
- Identify customer segments
- Assess size of market that can be reached
- Determine competitors' threats
- Identify what success factors need to be found out
- Ensure consistent core product which can be adjusted if needed
- What features/benefits can be offered to new customers?
- Why should they change to us?

	Action	Budget	Date	Responsibilities
Strategic Option 3 (continued) ● Can we change distribution channels and gain competitive advantage – improved service – lowered cost? ● Price sensitivity in each market segments according to prices you can get ● Determine objectives for prices, eg market presentation or niche specialist ● Determine best promotional strategy for each market segment ● Direct mail, personal contact referrals etc ● Determine financial limits for cost prospecting each new client ● Develop a budget for marketing effort				

- Calculate break-even sales level needed to recoup investment in marketing
- Determine reward mechanisms for sales effort
- Set goals for sales
- Ensure good internal communication as well as effective outward communication
- Recruitment/retention policies in marketing/sales as well as in support services
- Can internal systems cope with growth in sales?

Strategic Option 4 (see Chapter 5)
Diversification
- Justify why diversification is really necessary
- Establish reduction plans through team building
- Find products/services
- Network widely to find new customers

	Action	Budget	Date	Responsibilities
Strategic Option 4 (continued) • Assess joint return • Acquisition prospects • Sell out to someone else • Merger businesses • Collaborate				
Step 4. Can we do it?	**Action**	**Budget**	**Date**	**Responsibilities**
• Information systems needed. These should be integrated into each of the options discussed in Step 3. • Special needs which have hidden impact • Regular information needed for internal systems • Regular information needed from external sources				

Step 5. 'What if' analysis	Action	Budget	Date	Responsibilities
In choosing the options described above you will need to consult widely • List the people, institutions, publications and events from which you will source ideas, contacts and criteria for selecting your option				

Step 6. Financial implications	Action	Bdget	Date	Responsibilities
Financial implications have been taken into account but you may need to establish key success functions, for example: • Break-even levels • Contribution margin • Liquidity ratios • Performance measures • Profitability				

	Action	Budget	Date	Responsibilities
Step 6. Financial implications (continued) ● Payback and return on investment ● Risk/return objectives				
Step 7. Impact on personnel	**Action**	**Budget**	**Date**	**Responsibilities**

The human resource implication may also be wider than the pursuit of the strategic options leading you to consider:
● Personal goals
● Managerial styles
● Delegation needs
● Overall skills mix
● Job roles
● Personnel policies
  – recruitment
  – retention				

Step 7. Impact on personnel (continued)
- rewards
- health and safety
- pensions
- payment terms
- training plans

Step 8. Completing the plan	Action	Budget	Date	Responsibilities
The whole of this schedule is, of course, Step 8, the final piece of the jigsaw being the establishment of contingency plans. What if events do not go according to plan? Can you: ● Change direction ● Alter customer base ● Alter products ● Be flexible about prices ● Increase creativity and innovation ● Alter promotion/communication methods ● Train or alter staff?				

Index